ANDRA FISCHGRUND STANTON

FOREWORD BY SCOTT ROTH

CONTEMPORARY PHOTOGRAPHY
BY JAYE R. PHILLIPS

**STUDIO PHOTOGRAPHY
BY ADDISON DOTY**

MUSEUM OF NEW MEXICO PRESS   SANTA FE

Zapotec weavers

OF TEOTITLAN

To Marty, *un diseño especial*

Project editor: Mary Wachs
Art direction and design: David Skolkin
Composition: Set in Horley Old Style with Serpentine display
Manufactured in Hong Kong

10 9 8 7 6 5 4 3 2 1

Library of Congress Cataloging-in-Publication Data
Stanton, Andra Fischgrund.
   Zapotec weavers of Teotitlan / by Andra Fischgrund Stanton : field photographs
by Jaye Phillips.
   p. cm.
     Includes bibliographical references.
     ISBN 0-89013-333-6. -- ISBN 0-89013-334-4 (pbk.)
1. Zapotec weavers—Mexico—Teotitlan del Valle. 2. Zapotec textile fabrics—Mexico—
Teotitlan del Valle. 3. Hand weaving—Mexico—Teotitlan del Valle—Themes, motives. 4. Hand
weaving—Mexico—Teotitlan del Valle—Patterns. I. Title.
    F1221.Z3S68 1999   99-17988
    746.1'4'097274—dc21   CIP

Museum of New Mexico Press
Post Office Box 2087
Santa Fe, New Mexico 87504

CONTENTS

FOREWORD
BY SCOTT ROTH

This book is the first ever to present the story of the weavings of Teotitlán del Valle. This is a surprising fact given that Teotitlán has a two-thousand-year-old history as an important center of Zapotec culture and a blanket weaving tradition dating back to the earliest colonial period. These are the venerable foundations for the emergence, and prominence, of its colorful rugs in the world market today.

In my twenty-five years of living among and working alongside the weavers of Teotitlán, I have come to appreciate a great many things about their culture. Prominent for me is a customary graciousness in all the weavers' social exchanges, a quality that seems to contribute to the Teotitecos' vitality and that actually can be seen reflected in their craft.

While walking along the village's streets, the formality of greeting everybody one passes as a sign of respect is something that impresses me. That customary acknowledgment is even more pronounced in greeting one of a dozen or more grandparents and godparents. When such an individual is encountered in town, his or her hands are held and kissed. It was only two generations ago that all of one's elders were greeted in this manner.

Another major aspect of Teotitlán's gracious way of life is expressed through the festivals held nearly every week throughout the year. As invited guests, couples visit family member's homes to celebrate a patron saint, baptism, marriage, or funeral. These are grand events where the couples contribute to the preparation of large meals and, like everyone else present, enjoy a strong social connection through talking, drink-

opposite:
Teotitlán del Valle's six thousand villagers communally own some twenty thousand acres of virgin forest, rivers, and streams.

ing, and dancing. These are times of nurturing all-important ties among immediate and extended family members, neighbors, and friends as well as reconciling misunderstandings that often occur in a tight-knit community.

It is out of these social interactions that the Zapotec weavers seem to develop a sense of well-being and belonging, of being a valuable part of their community. It is from this self-confidence that such a large number of weavers find the creative reserves to develop their unique palettes and designs for their ever-evolving tapestries and rugs. The energy, enthusiasm, and sense of friendly competition they bring to the market seem to spring from this place of emotional and spiritual comfort.

Much like the city-states of medieval Italy, Teotitlán is a fairly autonomous social, economic, and political entity. Dialect, customs, and even physical traits distinguish its people from the neighboring townships. Teotitecos are very proud of the fact that their *sarapes* have been regarded as the finest woven blankets in all of southern Mexico during the last three hundred years, and they identify with the fact that their town was an administrative center for much of the Oaxaca Valley during that period as well.

There is historical irony in the comparison of Teotitlán to the other traditional *sarape* weaving centers, Tlaxcala and Texcoco. The industrial boom of the 1950s around Mexico City led many weavers in those locales to abandon their craft for better wages. Consequently, Teotitlán remained the only major colonial-period blanket weaving center in the country to survive into modern times, subsisting in an essentially pre-industrial economy into the 1960s. When the American market for handwoven textiles expanded in the 1980s, Teotitlán, because of the lack of more profitable employment, was still creating traditional weavings, with many enthusiastic young men prepared to present a body of work to the marketplace. The irony is that Teotitlán now has the highest standard of living of any native village in Mexico.

Men over fifty refer to the cashless economy prior to the 1960s when they recall how, as boys, they would take a handful of their family's corn to the market to exchange it for a necessary household item. To this day many of the utilitarian items found in village homes are locally handmade.

Perhaps it is that the weavers use simple, basic, understandable technologies in everything they create that accounts, ultimately, for the appeal of their tapestries and rugs. For unlike other rugs that seem almost too "perfect," Zapotec weavings hold the charm of springing from a life lived close to nature and close to community. No wonder they touch something in so many of us who are used to living cerebral lives in high-tech societies where we feel disconnected from the origins of most everything we use and where we pursue work that sometimes seems lacking in human scale.

Zapotec Weavers of Teotitlán provides valuable insights both for the collector of Zapotec rugs and for those who will someday make the journey to Teotitlán. The spectrum of weavings presented ideally will lead one to relish every further development of the Teotitecos' distinctive artisan tradition. If fortunate enough to visit some of the weavers' home workshops off the main streets, one will find the families willing to sincerely extend themselves with their time and hospitality. Through reading this book, I hope you will come to appreciate, as I have, the artistry and traditions of these very gracious people.

INTRODUCTION

The universe must have been smiling on us the day my husband and I first arrived in Oaxaca, Mexico. Within an hour of our arrival we providentially met a Zapotec Indian who for the last three years has been our guide, interpreter, Spanish teacher, business partner, and friend.

That day we met Felipe Hernández. Though working at the crafts store he co-owns in Oaxaca City, he hails from a village of weavers called Teotitlán del Valle some twenty-two miles to the east. Teotitlán's approximately six thousand residents trace their roots to the ancient Zapotec people, one of the first groups to settle in Central America. These days all of Teotitlán's citizens are in some way involved in its illustrious textile industry.

To enter the world of Zapotec weavings is to be pitched into a universe of color and texture, a visual feast. Everywhere in Teotitlán skeins of freshly dyed yarns, warmed by the sun, are drying against rough adobe walls. Their endless shades of purple, blue, red, orange, and green compel you to come close and feel the thick, nubby strands doused in heady mixtures of flower blossoms, leaves, and moss. This intoxicating panorama fills one's senses and casts a joyous, magical spell.

As far back as 500 B.C., Teotitlán's early weavers used cotton and the backstrap tension loom, still employed today in numerous Indian villages. They wove primarily for themselves and possibly for trade. Hundreds of years later, when the Aztec controlled much of Mexico, cloth was taken as tribute payments. In the 1500s the Spanish imposed levies as well, which the Zapotec weavers paid in the form of fabric and dyestuff.

Sunday market at Tlacolula

1

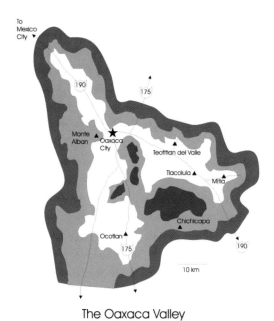

The Oaxaca Valley

When the Spanish seized Mexico in the early sixteenth century, they recognized Teotitlán's potential as a weaving center. Rather than dismantle the culture there as they did in so many areas of New Spain, they instead compelled native laborers to weave for the Spanish colonies. To augment textile production at Teotitlán, the Spanish invested in its modernization with the fixed-frame pedal loom, the loom most used today. This device enabled the weavers to work faster, create larger weavings, and switch from cotton to wool, which was also introduced by the Spanish.

This historical legacy ultimately would propel the Zapotec Indians of Teotitlán del Valle into national recognition and world renown. At the town market today, tourists congregate and dicker for the lowest prices, and even modestly talented weavers object when pressed for a bargain. For the best weavers, the market extends far beyond visiting tourists; their weavings sell to museums, galleries, and elite craft shops through international importers and distributors.

This book tells the story of an extraordinary community and a phenomenal people who have not only survived but prospered despite centuries of European subjugation and national strife. It presents Felipe Hernández and a legion of other weavers who create textiles of rare beauty out of the raw materials of nature. Moreover, it describes the skills of the women who card and spin some of the finest yarns imaginable and so make the weavers' textiles possible. Finally, it also chronicles the influence of the importers from the United States who opened up a market for these exceptional products, enabling the Zapotec community to achieve a modicum of material comfort in a poverty-stricken country.

Located two hundred miles southeast of Mexico City, Teotitlán del Valle is in Oaxaca, which has as many as fourteen linguistically distinct indigenous groups and ranks among the poorest of the country's thirty-one states. Oaxaca's subsistence farmers produce the staples of the local Indian diet that have persisted for millennia—squash, black beans, and corn. Many commute daily to their farms by burro and employ oxen and hand-hewn wooden plows to prepare their fields for planting.

Sometimes little more than tin walls and a roof, some homes in the state still lack plumbing and electricity. Many children grow up poorly fed and illiterate, with a large percentage dying each year of gastrointestinal illness and malnutrition. Alcoholism and drug abuse ravage both adults and children, especially in families torn apart by illness, disability, or death. Few economic safety nets exist, and families must rely on each other and on their communities to survive.

However, despite poverty and degradation, the people of Oaxaca possess a wealth of artistic inspiration. Throughout the state, daily and weekly markets showcase handi-

Before Dominican friars gave Mexico the fixed-frame pedal loom, Indians used the backstrap tension loom, or *telar de cintura*, still in use by countless weavers today.

crafts that attest to uncommon spirit and imagination. Besides textiles, products include green-glazed and black pottery, punched and painted tin, woven *rebozos* (shawls), embroidered *huipiles* (blouses), painted animal carvings, earthenware jugs, and tooled leather.

The pulse of Oaxaca is clearly its capital. Located at an elevation of five thousand feet in the state's central valley, Oaxaca City is one of Mexico's loveliest colonial cities. At once sophisticated and provincial, it functions as both a tourist mecca and a recreation and trading center for the surrounding pueblos. Teotitlán's weavers first came here to sell their wares in the 1950s when the new Pan-American Highway provided Mexican nationals with easier access to this crafts hub.

The city's main plaza, or *zócalo*, offers a kaleidoscopic scene of families picnicking beside fountains, musicians playing marimba music from the ornate bandstand, pushcart vendors hawking such local favorites as toasted grasshoppers in chile powder and lime juice, women selling fresh gardenias and calla lilies, and Trique Indian women seated on blankets weaving intricate designs with primitive backstrap looms.

Oaxaca is a land of contrasts, of artistic riches and dispiriting poverty, over which Teotitlán is balanced, for now, like a tightrope walker. Beneath it lie the traditions of its ancestors juxtaposed somewhat uncomfortably with the recent resourceful exploitation of the world beyond its borders. Though Teotitlán in large part owes its prosperity to the United States, repeated exposure to American ways could well prove to be its undoing. It will be on the shoulders of the emerging generation to manage its prosperity without falling prey to the forces that could tempt it from its cultural mainstays.

But the people of Teotitlán are resilient and may well defy the odds. Through the mutable currents of time, they have shown themselves to be able contortionists, discovering ways of adapting to changing local, national, and foreign pressures while all the while enjoying the success of their labors. Their weavings express the determination of a courageous people committed to the integrity of their artistry and to the continuity of their traditions.

top:
A complex system of weekly markets has been the lifeline for Oaxacans since Spanish colonial times. Each village's market showcases a special product, such as cheese, livestock, pottery, basketry, or weavings. Teotitlán's weavers first traded and sold their weavings at markets like this one, in Tlacolula, known for its agricultural produce and crafts.

bottom:
Teotitlán's children will be the next generation of weavers.

CHAPTER 1
WEAVING A CULTURE

In Teotitlán del Valle, many homes consist of a series of rooms surrounding a central courtyard, with cement, tile, or dirt floors and plastered walls washed in violet, rose, and peach. Typically, one room of the house is set aside as the devotional space for the home altar. Here, a table or shelf supports a painting or figurine of Mexico's patroness, the Virgin of Guadalupe. Candles and real or artificial flowers surround her image and those of patron saints. Members of the family decorate such altars and make offerings at fiesta time or to the saints in times of need. It is here in this room that the weavers store their completed rugs—the fruits of their devotion to tradition—and where their guests are shown their latest creations.

Virtually every home in Teotitlán is a showcase for weavings of extraordinary diversity and beauty. One weaver's rugs variously display playful depictions of birds, butterflies, fish, or turtles while another's quietly present a subdued natural palette in refined elegance. The designs encompass a wide range of imagery, from the stepped frets and lacy interlocking channels of the carved stone facades of ancient Mitla to Navajo geometrics and Ye'ii corn spirit figures to prehistoric antelope pictographs and modernist paintings by Miró, Picasso, and Rivera. Historical weaving motifs are reprised in contemporary Saltillo *sarapes*, and original patterns celebrate cosmic connection through "spirit messengers" and "gods' eyes."

In Teotitlán, tourists have the opportunity to appreciate the various elements and stages of weaving. Weavers frequently display ingredients of dyes and samples of colored yarns produced from them. Often they demonstrate the weaving process, creating several new lines of color by passing a shuttle through the warp of an unfinished rug on

Felipe Hernández winding up skeins of yarn.

a loom. All around them, visitors can see the results of the weavers' creative efforts: piles of riotously colored textiles stacked on benches and tables against the cool walls of altar rooms.

In the courtyard of Felipe Hernández's family home, a single prolific lime tree stands amid clucking chickens, a car in need of repairs, a spinning wheel, baskets of colored yarn, and six wooden looms. Born in 1962, Felipe has been weaving since age thirteen. In his family, as in most village families, the skills of carding, spinning, dyeing, and weaving wool have been passed down from generation to generation. When his father was young, selling or trading woven goods enabled a family to eke out a living. After Felipe's grandfather died from a fall in the village school, where he worked to supplement the family's income, Felipe's father obtained a visa and went to the United States to work as a day laborer. When not working the fields there, he farmed the family's own land, where he still grows corn, chick-peas, and black beans. These days he occasionally can be seen at a loom, looking older than his years.

Through good fortune, Felipe has been able to support his own family largely with money he earned after a buyer from the United States discovered his rugs and for the next ten years came regularly to Mexico to purchase them.

Such early good fortune gave Felipe a taste for the American dollar. As a result, he transformed himself into an entrepreneur any capitalist could respect: he sells weavings from his family's home; co-owns a handicraft shop; conducts tours of the pueblos and archaeological sites surrounding Oaxaca City; works with shop owners in the United States to produce custom-made rugs; and is considering establishing a rental car business. When he has surplus funds after paying for his family's necessities, Felipe pumps his money into a new home he is having built, which he hopes someday to turn into a bed-and-breakfast to augment his income. His dream, he says, is to retire young and travel around the world. He has already visited more parts of the United States than most North Americans.

Felipe weaves five hours a day, from four to nine every morning. Sometimes, if his tour guide service is slow, he weaves longer hours. Proud of his work, he considers himself an artist and insists that if he had an opportunity for another life, he would still be first and foremost a weaver. Felipe's life trajectory resembles that of many other weavers his age in that he no longer must work on his family's farm. Although once Teotitecos both farmed and produced crafts, currently only 10 percent farm full-time (Stephen 1991). Weavers who engage in farming as a secondary occupation spend an average of just three to four weeks per year in the fields in contrast to the daily labor of full-time farmers.

In this town of artisans, weaving businesses continue to consist primarily of immediate family members. Sons and daughters card yarn when they are youngsters

Demetrio Bautista is not only an expert weaver but owns a restaurant and a furniture factory. He is only one example of the many talented and energetic members of this extraordinary community.

and begin weaving as teenagers under the tutelage of their father. Fathers typically create the designs and dyes for the unique color palette that distinguishes each family's work.

With the growth of the industry, other production units have emerged. Some families hire additional weavers, including extended family and unrelated individuals, paying them by the piece. Commonly, one family member who is especially gifted with design or color will mentor the others. Demetrio Bautista is one such person. Talented in many areas, he not only teaches other weavers how to use the jewel-tone palette he has developed but has opened a restaurant as well as a furniture factory to supply his restaurant with beautiful pine tables and chairs.

A significant number of families employ dozens of weavers, sometimes from other towns, to produce rugs in great quantity for importers from the United States with multiple customers and large distribution areas. This arrangement benefits weavers in Teotitlán and arguably has helped raise the standard of living in neighboring towns such as Santa Ana and San Miguel, though it is said that Teotitecos can be exacting employers.

According to Francisco Toledo, one of Mexico's most famous artists, there was an attempt to establish weaving cooperatives in the late 1960s. Through workshops on

A pattern develops as the weaver adds new lines of color (weft threads) to the warp. Demetrio Bautista's weaving illustrates a serrated diamond design with an unusual zigzag border.

At eighty-four, Ponciano Hipolito is Teotitlán's oldest weaver still producing large pieces. He poses here with a small *Caracol* (Snail) weaving, a family design that his eight-year old grandson wove.

color, design, and technique, weavers with promise were to develop and further refine the craft, but the concept never took hold, perhaps because workshop organizers did not take into account the strength of familial bonds and the competitiveness of village families (Toledo 1998).

Unlike mass-production businesses, Felipe's relatively small operation only includes his parents, his wife and sons, and some extended family members. Still, there are six looms in his father's house, and his new home, under construction, contains three more, one of which can accommodate a ten-foot-wide rug. Like all the town's looms, Felipe's are built of pine by villagers, who then mount them on four posts and fashion them as tablelike structures. Even with constant use, looms can last up to a hundred years, though they require many repairs.

In the weaving process, uncolored warp (foundation) threads are wound around two rollers on either end of the tablelike structure. To operate the loom, the weaver stands at one end and begins the design by passing bobbins of colored yarn resting in a wooden "boat," or shuttle, through the warp threads. As the weaving progresses, the weaver turns the closest roller so that the textile forms a cylinder around it. In this way more new warp threads become available for weaving from the roller farthest away from the weaver. When the weaver steps on a floor pedal, every other warp thread lifts from the table. After each pass of the shuttle, the second set of warp threads lifts, and a pattern like the lattice of a fruit pie forms. Periodically, the artist pulls a batten, or comb, against the woven threads in order to compress them and produce a tight weave.

When a weaver is making a simple striped pattern, the shuttle flies rapidly across the width of the weaving and is passed back again. However, for complicated patterns, bobbins must be changed with each color variation. To do this, the weaver counts out and lifts up a number of warp threads, according to the design, and pulls the bobbin under. Thus, complex designs are extremely time-consuming and take a toll on the weaver's back and legs.

Once a weaving is completed, it is cut loose from the loom and scraped with a metal scraper to smooth the surface and remove burrs and other organic matter in the wool. Finally, the warp threads are tied together, usually to form braided or twisted fringe. A select group of weavers further refines the textile by weaving these warp threads back into the piece or sewing a braid over its edges.

Many families in Teotitlán are known for the unique colors of their weavings. Zacarias Soza uses a harmonious blend of jewel tones and undyed fleece tones while

Antonio Martínez employs brilliant natural and aniline dyes that have made his tapestries so fiercely sought after. Other weavers known for their expert colors include Manuel Montaño and Zacarias Ruíz, who use attractive reds, blues, and greens; Braulio Lazo, one of the first weavers to develop a broad palette of compatible pastels; and Bulmaro Pérez, who employs claret red, caramel yellow, and aubergine dyes. Only in his twenties, Pérez is causing a sensation in U.S. rug markets. Seven years ago he created his first colors, using gray wools as a base. Since then he has perfected his complex recipes, which often involve combining several different dyes for each color.

As for Felipe Hernández, he expertly produces rose, blueberry, and peach but also has the distinction of being one of the few weavers in town who dyes yarns for custom orders. Through considerable trial and error, he became knowledgeable about matching colors to customers' tastes. He says of this process, "It is very hard and takes a great deal of time, but I like it. I like to learn. It gives me an opportunity to think of new possibilities."

As Felipe continues to acquire knowledge about the intricacies of weaving production, he teaches his three sons the traditions of his forefathers. Each one knows how to card and spin wool and how to weave. Although two have become expert weavers in their own right, Felipe hopes his children will eventually pursue other careers and engage in weaving only as a secondary vocation; he wants them to have an easier life than his own. His eldest son, Victor, girl-crazy at age nineteen, has graduated from secondary school but so far has no interest in continuing his education. That he has not chosen a profession causes Felipe concern. On the other hand, his middle son, Eric, wants to be a mechanic and will attend trade school while his youngest son, Jorge, longs to be an airline pilot after going to college. To help them achieve their goals, Felipe pays for private high school in Oaxaca City and acts as a chauffeur for his sons every evening when school is out.

Despite continuing ancient traditions, most families in Teotitlán experience conflict between traditional ways and modern life. For now, weaving is a time-honored and lucrative activity but results in a hard life. However, with increasing exposure to the luxuries of wealthy Americans, Europeans, and Mexicans, weavers yearn for a more

Wilebaldo Bazán, sixty-two, started weaving traditional *sarapes* in the 1940s with his father. Today he specializes in intricately patterned rugs.

affluent life-style. Every day they encounter juxtapositions of the old and the new, with new ways compelling and sometimes seductive or confusing. For example, while his father rides a burro to the family farm, Felipe greets tourists arriving by jet. In certain areas of town, fax machines and compact disc players hum in houses with no plumbing or running water.

Considering both the beauty resulting from ancient customs and the difficulty of people's daily lives, it is hard to know what to hope for. Change, nonetheless, is happening. Today, for the first time in Zapotec history, children are raised in a cash economy and educated through the sixth grade. Their world has been considerably expanded through television and constant exposure to foreign travelers. If they eventually forsake weaving for less labor-intensive jobs, the local textile industry will inevitably feel the impact. It will be for the next generations to determine the future of the weaving industry.

For now, though, Teotitecos enjoy the fruits of their weaving legacy. History suggests they will find ways to adapt to the changing world around them without losing sight of their roots. It is likely they will once again discover inventive directions that incorporate the old and the new since it is tradition that maintains their sense of identity and their creativity. As Felipe says, "When I am in the United States I am not treated well. People look at me as one more poor, stupid Mexican. But in my village people respect me as I respect them. Our heritage sustains us. We all have something to contribute. I will never leave Teotitlán."

Jesús Hernández

Jesús Hernández is Felipe's neighbor and good friend. The second of nine children, he is forty-six years old. His siblings and parents live in Mexico City, having left Teotitlán thirty years ago for access to better schools and jobs. In those days villagers had difficulty surviving financially because only locals were buying the blankets and ponchos they produced. Five of his brothers and sisters abandoned weaving to become factory workers while the other three entered the fields of dentistry, engineering, and sales. They visit their hometown frequently, and Jesús makes them weavings for their houses in the city.

Jesús began learning the craft of weaving when he was ten years old, taught by his father to prepare bobbins and later to card and spin raw wool into yarn. At twelve he made his first rug. When he married, his father-in-law set him up in business in town. Now he owns a homestead on the road into town, complete with a showroom. On the shady porch, his wife weaves a complicated pattern on a small loom while nearby a family member creates a rug of undyed wools.

In the area between house and showroom, Jesús locates his well, spinning wheel, grinding stone, and metal tubs for dyeing yarn. Hundreds of years ago Zapotec weavers discovered how to create colorfast dyes using indigenous plants, minerals, and insects. Though the techniques were lost for a time with the introduction of synthetic dyes, the weavers revived them when they realized the market valued the more traditional methods.

When first invented in the 1850s, synthetic dyes enabled weavers to expand their color palettes (Klein 1997: 70) with bright, color-saturated yarns in colors not found in nature. An added benefit was the relative ease of buying prepared dyes in the village market where before they bore the burden of trekking into the mountains to gather wild plants. Yet although synthetic dyes enriched color schemes, they did not produce the subtle shades obtainable with natural dyes, prompting some weavers to reject the synthetics. Today, most weavers are more skillful at manipulating aniline dyes to realize more pleasing hues and so take a pragmatic view regarding their use. They feel it is much easier and more time-efficient to use aniline dyes for large orders while for small or custom orders they select whichever dyes will result in the desired effect.

The range of colors derived from natural dyes is impressive. Jesús has a collection of vegetable dye ingredients that he shows to customers. They include alfalfa leaves for green dyes; pomegranate skin or rock moss for yellow dyes; pods from *huizache* (a kind of acacia) for black dyes; indigo leaves for blue dyes; bougainvillea blossoms for pink dyes; nut tree bark for brown dyes; and pecan shells for tan dyes.

An unexpected substance produces red dyes: the crushed larvae of the cochineal insect (*Dactylopius coccus*) (Ross 1986). This parasite, which attacks certain species of prickly pear and nopal cactus, was called *nochezti* by the Aztec Indians, meaning "blood of the cactus" (Sayer 1985). Crushing the larvae yields a striking crimson hue. In the recent past, cochineal had to be imported from Peru despite the fact that during the colonial era it once was a major Oaxacan product exported to Spain. When natural dyes lost their popularity, local people no longer cultivated it, and weavers could only find it on wild cactus plants in the mountains.

Today, however, a cochineal farm in the Oaxaca Valley, established in the 1980s,

top:
Using a wooden loom built in town, María Elena Mendoza begins her design by throwing a shuttle across the length of the loom.

bottom:
In carding wool, raw fleece is straightened, aligned, and softened as two paddles with metal teeth are scraped across it. Though not difficult, this procedure is time-consuming and tiring.

Although most weavers say they employ them, in fact only about a dozen families regularly and expertly utilize the natural dyes.

top right:
Alicia Vásquez uses a traditional grinding stone, or *metate*, to pulverize the cochineal larvae, about seventy thousand of which are needed to produce one pound of dye powder.

bottom right:
Along an ancient path, Eligio Bazan carries freshly dyed cochineal yarn to the Quieliunteo River, at the base of Teotitlán's watershed, for rinsing.

Eligio Bazan's mother, Magdalena Martínez, boils wool in a cochineal dye bath. After four hours, when the maximum dye density has been reached, the yarns will be removed and rinsed of excess color.

sells this dye, which is quite expensive at about $50 per pound, or seventy thousand insects. Here, rows of nopal cactus pads are planted in sandy soils and protected from the elements by plastic tarps. On the pads workers "seed" a female insect; eventually a white powder along with tiny reddish brown larvae cover the surface. A wax-based secretion, the powder protects the larvae from desiccation in the semiarid climate. After approximately one hundred days, the larvae reach maturity and the cactus pads are pulled from the soil. They are first scraped into boiling water then spread over drying shelves, where they remain for several weeks. Finally, they are bagged for sale. The cactus pads are then replanted, and the cycle is repeated.

Jesús's wife, Alicia Vásquez, demonstrates how they prepare dye from cochineal larvae. First, she pours tiny gray granules from a plastic bag containing the dried larvae. Next, using a kind of rolling pin, she sits on the ground before her *metate*, or grinding stone, and slowly and methodically crushes the larvae, causing the implements and her hands to turn purple.

In half an hour, Alicia has transformed half a pound into powder. She than collects the cochineal in a bowl and rinses the metate, being careful to catch the runoff since cochineal is too valuable to waste. Jesús then stirs the macerated cochineal into a tub of boiling water over a fire fueled by tree limbs. To this mixture, he adds lime halves (*limón seca*), salt, and *tejute* leaves—all natural dye mordants that help the yarn absorb color. Then the yarn is immersed in the liquid and, when it has reached the desired color—usually after several hours—removed. The dye bath can be used a second time, but it will produce a lighter hue; it can also be utilized to overdye yarn that has already been dyed to create unusual colors. In another tub, Jesús prepares blue dye by soaking small pellets of dried, compressed indigo leaves in an alkaline solution of lime, wood, and ashes. After three or four days, the pellets attain a doughlike consistency and will dissolve in boiling water.

The dyeing process preceding weaving is very time-consuming. The couple leaves skeins of yarn in the dye for days and sometimes weeks, depending on the desired shade. Afterward they wash and wring out the yarn, sometimes in mountain streams, then dry it on clotheslines in the sun. Once dry, they wind the skeins onto bobbins in preparation for weaving.

Many husbands and wives undertake the laborious dyeing process together. Even before the dyeing, yarn must be washed with soap to remove vegetation and dirt, then hung to dry. And after dyeing, it has to be washed again four or five times. Preparation of yarn for an average-size rug can easily take many days.

Jesús and Alicia weave three hours in the morning and another

top:
Depending on the plant dye used, skeins of wool yarn sometimes steep in dye baths for days or weeks.

bottom:
One of the natural dyes revived during the 1960s, indigo takes the form of dried paste pellets harvested in the Isthmus region of Oaxaca, 150 miles southeast of Teotitlán.

Felipe Hernández, and Maria Elena Mendoza dye yarn using aniline dyes and sulfuric acid, a caustic process that exposes the weavers to dangerous chemicals.

bottom:
At El Rancho la Nopalera in Coyótepec, programs promote the use of cochineal to the region's weaving industry. The farm also sells dried cochineal larvae, shown here on cactus pads. Photo by Marcela Taboada.

three hours in the afternoon. At other times of the day in the dry season they wait on customers while during the planting and growing season Jesús labors raising corn and chick-peas on the twelve acres of land he inherited from his father. Like most weavers, Jesús uses the proceeds from textile sales to purchase family necessities.

Jesús devotes a great deal of thought to his textile designs, especially color placement. On the smooth stone floor of his showroom, he lays out a handsome Navajo-inspired weaving and explains that to be visually pleasing patterns of color must flow from light to medium to dark. He listens patiently though skeptically to other ideas. The success of his theory is demonstrated most beautifully by his undyed rugs, made of wool naturally tinted in tones of brown, gray, tan, yellow, and cream.

Like many weavers in Teotitlán, Jesús is profoundly religious. He claims that God provides the faith he has in the land to produce food and in the rain to make it grow. Motioning to his heart, he remarks, "My religion is deep inside me. It teaches me to respect others, to not be a bad person, to live together in peace—*convivir*. Religion, family, and community are the same for me."

Indeed, in Teotitlán religious piety and respect for family, friends, and neighbors are reflected in all community activities. Villagers exhibit gracious good manners when interacting, using soft-spoken greetings; shaking hands with both hands and a bowed head (or sometimes even kissing hands); making a great effort not to offend; and maintaining a respectful attitude as expressed through steady vocal inflection and nonaggressive body language (Selby 1974: 29).

Community service is central to the value system of the village and is considered a way of expressing mutual respect and humility. In fact, the town has a *cargo* system whereby villagers must "volunteer" time to take care of various aspects of community life (Stephen 1991: 161). Both men and women do their initial one- or two-year period of service as soon as they get married and another every five years, each requiring more experience and maturity. This service involves jobs such as policing one of the five regions in the village; developing or overseeing irrigation, fire fighting, electrical, and school systems; or maintaining bridges, streets, the museum, and the church. Moreover, a judicial branch of the system entails adjudicating property transfers and sales, local disputes, and family disagreements (Stephen 1991: 163). Even the position of mayor, which requires working six days a week for three years, is voluntary.

This system not only promotes community solidarity but has educational benefits as well. At any given time more than two hundred men and women of the town's six thousand residents fill such service roles. The more financially successful serve in the most important jobs since they have proved themselves to be good leaders and can better afford to give of their time. By serving those who are less successful or qualified, they learn humility. Moreover, during each period of volunteer work every person develops a kind of expertise, earning respect from other villagers for acquired knowledge and experience and thereby elevating that individual's status in the community. Thus, the system is a great equalizer, making all villagers feel valued and important (Roth 1998).

Such service also results in tangible improvements for the community. A paved road running from the Pan-American Highway to the town's center was a consequence

Sixty-five-year-old Vicente Gabriel runs a one-man weaving operation, performing all aspects of the weaving process himself, from preparing the yarn to weaving his designs. He still washes his weavings in amole root, an ancient process used to soften the fibers.

It is said that a fiesta is held every day of the year in Teotitlán. Some are elaborate and involve thousands of townspeople, such as the *Dios de los Muertos* (Days of the Dead) celebration. Others are smaller and more private. Here, Armando Hipolito and Aurea Dolores Gonzalez marry in the village church. Copal incense, candles, bouquets of calla lilies, and traditional songs from a local band create a magical atmosphere.

of such a commitment. Prior to this development, the community only had access to the highway via a dirt road through an adjacent town, Macuilxochitl. Another outgrowth of such volunteer work was the establishment of an outdoor textile market for tourists in 1985 (Stephen 1991: 141).

Perhaps because of community solidarity achieved through this system, Teotitlán has always fought to maintain a high degree of autonomy from the Mexican government. Weavers avoid providing accurate accounts of the weaving industry so that the state government does not find it financially lucrative enough to get involved in textile production.

Despite their strong desire for control over their community and their many accomplishments, there is more work to be done, especially to improve education. Even though it is now mandatory for children to attend school through the sixth grade (age thirteen) and in 1977 a new secondary school curriculum made it possible for them to study until age sixteen, there are no high schools in Teotitlán. Thus, only families who can afford the expense send their children to Oaxaca City and Mexico City for a secondary education.

Classes are taught in Spanish, although Teotitecos speak Zapotec, one of the fourteen distinct indigenous languages spoken in the state of Oaxaca, including Mixtec, Amuzgo, and Chatino. Zapotec survives only because families value it as part of their ethnic heritage and so pass it on to their children. Because Zapotec is a tonal language, in which inflection confers meaning, outsiders find it difficult to learn; and even among Indians the language has a different form in each of the many pueblos where it is spoken.

In spite of their difficult existence and the improvements needed in their village, most people of Teotitlán highly value the customs of the region. Jesús Hernández and his wife want their six children to have an easier life with less labor-intensive jobs, but they also want them to carry on weaving and other community traditions. Indeed, Jesús acknowledges that if he could begin life over again he would still wish to be a weaver living in his cherished Teotitlán.

Zoyla and Zenón Mendoza own one of the shops along Teotitlán's main street. Built in 1961, it stands out among all the stores with its high ceiling and huge rugs draping the massive clay walls. The cool air, the rich colors of the tapestries, and the sense of serenity all lend an almost religious ambience to this showroom.

Standing patiently among piles of rugs, Zoyla Mendoza is a small woman with a shy smile. Married for twelve years, she and her husband live with his parents ten blocks away. To escape the poor economic conditions in Teotitlán, Zoyla's family moved to Chicago when she was fifteen. There she worked in a luggage factory for four years. Although she enjoyed her life in the United States and wanted to stay, her father insisted she return with the family to their hometown.

Today, she says she has no regrets about coming back to Teotitlán. Her husband taught her to weave a few years ago, and she loves working on challenging designs. Women have always been weavers here but began to weave in earnest during the 1970s when production expanded as new markets opened up. Before that time, women traditionally carded, spun, and washed wool, in addition to their normal activities of raising children, managing the household, tending to farm animals, making tortillas and corn drinks to sell in local markets, and taking part in the religious ceremonies of the village.

When he is not helping his wife in their shop, Zenón Mendoza oversees the work of family members who produce textiles for the store. Yet every year, as a labor of love, he designs and weaves one or two special rugs that can take up to eight months to complete due to their complexity. One such rug is exceedingly intricate, consisting of almost a patchwork quilt of small rugs, each with numerous design elements, including stylized animals and geometric shapes. After finishing such a rug, Mendoza admits his back aches, but he goes without medical care because, he says, "The doctor will take all of our money."

In part because of his back pain, he dreads the day when he will be forced to work the family farm. Now his father grows the usual corn, black beans, and chick-peas for sale or in lean times for family use. Zoyla confirms that when her father-in-law passes away her husband will have to work the fields or else the family will lose its farm, adding, "He doesn't like the idea, but he has to do it."

The couple is concerned about how Teotitlán's growing population will affect land use. Although larger families need more and more land to survive as children grow up and want their own homes, available land is limited. The Mendozas are concerned that the local government will ask them to give up some of their land, which they feel would be unfair.

However, in general they approve of the way the village is run. In the 1930s, the mayor established postal service; in 1965, electricity was brought in; in 1975, piped water became available; and in the mid-1980s, telephone service began. More recently, the town's dirt roads are being paved. Zoyla remarks with amusement, "If the streets aren't kept clean, the mayor gets mad and makes you do extra community work!"

Zoyla Mendoza and her husband own a weaving shop on the main street of Teotitlán, where her family weaves a multitude of both simple and intricately patterned rugs. Señora Mendoza is also a celebrated cook in the village.

Teotitlán's fiesta celebrating the Precious Blood of Christ, the church's most venerated image, is held annually in July. It begins with a procession,depicted here, on the days leading up to the first Wednesday of the month. It is a time for the community to celebrate its complex Catholic tradition blending indigenous and European elements. The *senoritas* of the village, representing the prominent families of the church and town, highlight the parade in their costumes reminiscent of nineteenth-century fiesta dress with its embroidered blouse, hand-woven cochineal-dyed wool wrap skirt, raw silk sash, and rebozo.

It is said that every day somewhere in Teotitlán there is a celebration—a wedding, a birthday party, a national or local secular holiday, or a Catholic or Indian religious ceremony. "Every Sunday," Zoyla Mendoza declares with evident delight, "someone gets married!"

Elaborate arrangements are made for many of the celebrations. For example, weddings usually last two or three days, but preparation can take another month. They entail a ceremony, dancing, and several meals. The largest weddings, called *fandangos*, are often attended by more than three or four hundred townspeople. With a full brass band, ritual expressions of gratitude to animals that will be eaten at the feast, and bouquets of delicate red and white flowers made from sugar, such affairs reflect the villagers' reverence for tradition and great capacity for merriment (Mendoza 1998).

Because turning down an invitation to any wedding or birthday celebration is considered insulting and can lead to loss of relationships and respect, villagers divide their time between supporting the community and attending to their own needs (Mendoza 1998). Many women in particular view these invitations as a burden. Because they tend to do most of their family's work, they realize that accepting them assures continuation of community cooperation.

Zoyla Mendoza clearly enjoys such occasions and along with her husband has volunteered for six months to host a monthly community celebration to honor a saint associated with the town. Partly through such social activities, she has become a cooking expert, and her premier dish, *Tamales Amarillos*, has been written up in English- and Spanish-language magazines and cookbooks. The fiesta the Mendozas plan to host will require many months of preparation, including making candies, chocolate *atole* (a thick, warm drink made from finely ground corn), *mole* sauce (with as many as twenty ingredients such as chile peppers, cinnamon, tomatoes, pumpkin seeds, nuts, and bitter chocolate), tortillas, and, of course, *Tamales Amarillos*. However, despite the work involved Zoyla sees this as an important means of connecting to family and community. She says, "I never want to leave my village. I love the traditions. They keep me close to my family and to the town. I feel I am important here, and I am proud to be of service."

Plate 1
Lasero Montaño, 1977
Untitled
42 x 57 ins.

Pecan husks and zapote fruit provide for the natural dyes found in this original composition. The weft was handspun by the weaver's wife. Weaving courtesy of Scott Roth.

Plate 2
Ponciano Hipolito, 1998
Caracol (Snail)
24 x 36 ins.

A common pattern but woven here in an unusually small format. The dyes are aniline, and the yarn is handspun.

Plate 3
Manuel Montaño, 1998
Estrellas con Alas (Stars
with Wings)
48 x 78 ins.

This commercial design is
of factory wool and vivid
colors from aniline dyes.

Plate 4
Bulmaro Pérez, 1998
Persia
40 x 70 ins.

Pérez has taken a classic
Persian central motif and
added a playful border of
triangles. The rug is ani-
line-dyed factory wool.

CHAPTER TWO
THE LEGACY OF ZAPOTEC WEAVERS

A bumpy and crumbling thoroughfare in this part of the country, the Pan-American Highway winds its way to a sign for Teotitlán del Valle that promises, "We Have the Best Prices!" Twenty minutes from Oaxaca City, Teotitlán lies in a valley stretching out to the Sierra Madre del Sur Mountains. From May to October, rains bathe the surrounding fields and hills, turning them green and fertile.

Approaching the town, brick and adobe homes dot the grasslands, with enticing rugs fluttering on their porches. Gradually the countryside recedes, and the town's main street appears, with its new cobblestone sidewalks and decorative plantings. Shops compete for the visitor's attention with brightly painted signs and colorful carpets hanging on doors. Everywhere local residents work feverishly to keep up with the demand for these celebrated textiles.

Though they live in one of the poorest states in the country, skill, ingenuity, and business acumen have enabled the Zapotec weavers of Teotitlán to achieve a relative prosperity. Here most residents enjoy electricity and pumped water, many own cars and trucks, and some have telephones and fax machines. The new generation heads off to college and nontraditional jobs. Everywhere new and elaborate homes and storefronts rise from once-vacant land or from previous, more modest structures. This community on the move revels in the golden age of its weaving industry.

Teotitlán, which dates to pre-Columbian times, has had an elevated status throughout Mexico's history. Considered by Zapotec Indians to be the site where their sun-god gave oracles, Teotitlán was called Xa-Guia, or "beneath the stone," in reference to a mountain peak where the deity entered his temple. Not far from there the first Zapotec city, Monte Albán, emerged and flourished, taking Zapotec culture to new heights.

Near Oaxaca's airport the mysterious pyramidal outcroppings of Monte Albán spreading across a flat mountaintop rise up through the mist. Silent now, this once bustling metropolis was home to an elite group of lords and ladies, priests and warriors, who ruled a vast empire. All around them, along the gently sloping hills of the Sierra Juárez Mountains and in the valley below, farmers, intellectuals, and artisans worked to support the nobility's sumptuous life-style. It was here that the ancestors of Teotitlán's Zapotec Indians developed the weaving tradition that would ultimately give them international recognition.

Archaeologists believe that Monte Albán evolved from nomadic bands of native inhabitants who collected wild plants such as acorns, piñon nuts, mesquite beans, and prickly pear cactus and hunted game such as deer, cottontail rabbits, and mud turtles (Miller 1985: 5). Between 1500 and 1000 B.C., these people learned how to domesticate *teosinte*, a wild grass now known as Indian corn, or maize (Marcus and Flannery 1996: 66). Farming, aided by primitive irrigation, enabled them to eventually form small communities of three to ten households, which by 1000 B.C. had expanded to include several hundred households (Whitecotton 1977). As surpluses of agricultural resources accumulated, an emerging group of powerful community members began controlling and redistributing them to the rest of the populace, thus establishing an elevated status. This emerging elite class soon also commandeered exotic goods such as decorated pottery, magnetite mirrors, and seashells brought to towns such as San José Magote from neighboring areas, thus widening the gap between social classes (Sabloff 1997).

The aggregation of so many varied people spawned a high degree of creativity soon resulting in ceremonial architecture, a system of writing, and religious and solar calendars (Miller 1985: 28). Eventually, the nobility of Oaxaca's villages cooperatively established a central capital, perhaps to avoid warfare between developing hamlets or for a common defense against potential outside threats (Sabloff 1997: 50). They located Monte Albán on a secure mountaintop overlooking Oaxaca Valley, in an area with good soil and a climate suitable for year-round farming.

Much of what is known about life in Monte Albán has been gleaned from murals, stone carvings, and ceramic urns and figurines. From 500 B.C., and over the next five centuries, Zapotec society developed into a highly diversified culture, which besides the ruling classes included ballplayers, merchants, musicians, dancers, court jesters, jewelers, weavers, farmers, and slaves. In addition to a main plaza with monumental temples, a ball court, and an astronomical observatory, there were outlying residential areas. During the first few centuries of its existence, Monte Albán had about five thousand residents; by 200 B.C., the population had reached fifteen thousand and by A.D. 450 peaked at twenty-five thousand (Sabloff 1997: 56).

The inhabitants of the first Zapotec capital, Monte Albán, developed Mexico's first ceremonial architecture, hieroglyphic writing, and a sophisticated system of calendrics.

Teotitlán was primarily an agrarian society at this time, producing crops for its own consumption and for trade. Women, using native plants such as cotton (*Gossypium*) and maguey derived from the agave plant, wove cloth on the backstrap loom to meet the needs of family and possibly the requirements of the elite (Sayer 1985: 23). Their loom, known as the *telar de cintura*, was probably inspired by finger-weaving employed to make mats, netting, and baskets by the first immigrants to the New World

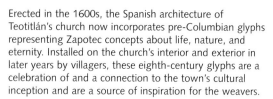

Erected in the 1600s, the Spanish architecture of Teotitlán's church now incorporates pre-Columbian glyphs representing Zapotec concepts about life, nature, and eternity. Installed on the church's interior and exterior in later years by villagers, these eighth-century glyphs are a celebration of and a connection to the town's cultural inception and are a source of inspiration for the weavers.

around 5000 B.C. (Sayer 1985: 21). It apparently evolved independently throughout South and Central America, where indigenous people continue to use it. Its distinctive feature is a system for supporting the warp, or foundation threads, so the threads are divided into two sets that are raised alternately, creating an opening through which the weaver passes weft threads.

Knowledge about textiles from the Monte Albán era is quite limited. Few textile artifacts from this era have survived due to moisture and other adverse conditions, and fragments that have been found in dry caves in Chiapas, for example, tell us little about their size or function. However, clay figurines, murals, carved stone glyphs, and codices (manuscripts on bark paper and deer hide) depicting native dress and everyday life provide clues about ancient customs (Sayer 1985: 15–16).

Such artifacts indicate that the uses of weavings reflected status in the community. Bracelets, brilliant feathers, and colorful cotton mantles, or capes, were reserved for the aristocracy while commoners could wear only drab garments made of agave plants. Archaeological findings suggest that some textiles from this period were quite complicated and diverse. Patterns inscribed in clay attest to the use in weavings of dots,

A page from the *Codex Nuttall*, an eleventh-century illustrated Mixtec manuscript showing the early uses of plain and decorated textiles.

These clay figurines, sporting geometrically adorned *huipiles* (blouses), date back to A.D. 600–900, Monte Albán's cultural florescence. Courtesy of the Howard S. Rose Gallery, Inc., New York.

crosses, stylized flowers, and stepped frets (Sayer 1985: 53). Clay stamps dipped in dyes may have been used to imprint designs. These stamp designs now serve as patterns for modern-day weavers.

Then, around A.D. 700 after centuries of prosperity, for unknown reasons this thriving metropolis began to disintegrate, its citizens settling in smaller city-states throughout the valley (Sabloff 1997: 56). Theories about the reason for Monte Albán's demise include the idea that external threats ceased to exist, thus reducing the need for protection, or that its population expanded beyond its agricultural limits.

Whatever the reason, the decline of Monte Albán soon created instability and turmoil. Smaller cities fought each other and invading groups, particularly the Mixtec and the Aztec. As the Mixtec gained power around A.D. 900, in return for protection the Zapotec were forced to pay tributes to them in the form of gold dust, fowl, slaves, and cotton cloth (Miller 1985: 28).

Five hundred years later, the Aztecs established a far-reaching empire that stretched from the Gulf Coast to the Pacific that included an estimated fifteen million people, among them the Zapotecs. All people in the empire were taxed in the form of goods, guaranteeing the Aztecs a never-ending supply of luxury items. Tribute lists show that Teotitlán was producing cotton cloth that was distributed as far away as the Aztec capital, Tenochtitlán. By 1500, the Aztecs had consolidated their authority, creating the most powerful state in the history of ancient Mexico (Miller 1985: 49).

In 1519, Spanish conquistadors and religious representatives arrived in Mexico and with the aid of the Tlaxcala Indians, who had long resisted Aztec domination, were able to defeat the Aztecs and establish authority. Religion was used to justify Spanish conquests. The conquerors sought to capture riches for the Crown and souls for the church. The clergy looked upon the Indians as wards, who were being delivered from idolatry and barbarism (Whitecotton 1977). The Indians accepted the new religion without abandoning their old beliefs; instead they combined the two theologies, which had similarities. Both stressed man's subservience to the supernatural; Catholic saints and Indian deities both had human attributes as well as miraculous powers of healing; and the bread and wine of Communion was akin to offerings of food to the dead for their journey throughout the underworld. Such fusion of religions, which scholars call syncretism, is still evident among the Zapotec Indians today (Whitecotton 1977).

In addition to converting the Zapotec Indians to Christianity, the Spanish coerced the native elite to work for the Crown while the rest of the populace was reduced to serving as a source of labor and commodities. The Spanish, like the Mixtec and Aztec, expected tribute payments from the Indians in the form of goods, referred to as *encomiendas* (Sayer 1985: 75). Further, a second system, a form of forced labor known as *repartimiento*, was instituted, enabling the Spanish to use the Indians as laborers for the church, Spanish estates, mines, and other economic enterprises (Miller 1985: 112).

In Teotitlán, the Zapotec Indians were forced to pay tributes in the form of cotton cloth. They were also obligated to collect vast numbers of cochineal insects for the production of red dye, requiring endless journeys into the mountains, where the insects are imbedded on the pads of wild nopal cactus. Thus, even though the conquistadors did not find the gold they had sought in Oaxaca, they turned cochineal into an alternative source of wealth. By the 1600s, the value of this commodity was second only to silver (Sayer 1985).

During this time the Zapotec population dwindled to 45,000 from 350,000 due largely to diseases for which the people had no immunity. At times, smallpox, plague, and measles killed three to four people each day in Teotitlán (Stephen 1991: 69).

As the conquistadors became richer and more independent, the Spanish Crown sought to restrict their power by imposing limits on tributes that could be exacted from the peasantry. In response, the conquerors claimed the land of the Indians and forced natives to become peons, or landless workers. Thus, the hacienda system was initiated whereby Indians were made to work the great sugar, tobacco, cacao, and indigo plantations for such low wages that they had to borrow from hacienda owners and consequently were obligated to them for the duration of their lives. Such avarice on the part of the conquistadors foreshadowed the nearly one hundred years of strife that were to characterize the period of Mexican history just before and following the 1846 Mexican War of Independence (Miller 1985).

Fortunately, during this period of colonization the people of Teotitlán were allowed to keep their lands. Moreover, the Spanish introduced new tools to the weaving trade that ultimately improved textile production and helped weavers survive. According to legend, the Dominican Bishop López de Zarate gave the Indians of Teotitlán the fixed-frame pedal loom, the spinning wheel, sheep, carding paddles, scissors, and steel needles, enabling the weavers to create a new product—the wool blanket. He also taught weaving classes to men in the village, who soon began to make textiles (Stephen 1991: 107).

The first Spanish invaders had brought with them churro sheep, which yielded thick wool suitable for blankets. Though several herds of soft-wooled merino sheep were later introduced in an attempt to improve, or perhaps replace, the churro breed, the experiment never succeeded. By the mid-seventeenth century, the churro wool blanket industry was well under way (Jeter and Juelke 1978: 19).

Although wool blanket production in Mexico was at first dominated by textile factories operated by slaves and modeled on those in Spain, by the end of the 1700s the Spanish had discovered that smaller workshops run by free Indians were less expensive to operate, and small-scale production, such as that in Teotitlán, became more prevalent. Thus, in the nineteenth century free workers most probably were responsible for the continuing growth of the weaving industry (Jeter and Juelke 1978: 19).

Plate 5
Isaac Vásquez, 1975
**The Spirit of a Woman
in a Butterfly**
41 x 57 ins.

This design was taken
from a fifth-century
Zapotec ceramic shard
found at Monte Albán.
The natural dyes were
used with factory- and
handspun yarn. Weaving
courtesy of Scott Roth.

Plate 6
Federico Chavez, 1998
Caracol (Snail)
48 x 78 ins.

Made with six shades
of undyed natural churro
fleece, the yarns were
hand-spun in Chichicapa
with an ancient drop-
spindle.

Plate 7
Ponciano Hipolito, 1981
Caracol (Snail)
33 x 55 ins.

This original composition is taken from a sixth-century pre-Columbian carving in Teotitlán's church. The dyes are aniline, and the weft was spun with a spinning wheel. Weaving courtesy of Scott Roth.

Plate 8
Herlinda Soza de
Gutiérrez, n.d.
Caracol (Snail)
38 x 66 ins.

Designed by the weaver's
husband, Ismael Gutiérrez,
this unusual design is dis-
tinguished by circular year
symbols adapted from the
Codex Nuttall. Weaving
courtesy of Scott Roth.

Plate 9
Isaac Vásquez, 1976
Mayan Bas Relief
43 x 48 ins.

The dyes for this weaving
are from pecan husks,
indigo, cochineal, rock
moss (yellow), and
huizache (black). The yarns
were spun with a spinning
wheel. This weaving is an
example of the expert use
of curvilinear forms, so difficult to execute on a
pedal loom. Weaving
courtesy of Scott Roth.

Plate 10
Zacarias Soza, 1982
Greca Original (Original
Zapotec Geometric)
38 x 69 ins.

A Zapotec pattern taken
from a carved eighth-cen-
tury glyph. This weaving
incorporates a wide range
of undyed fleece tones
with cochineal and indigo
dyes. Weaving courtesy of
Scott Roth.

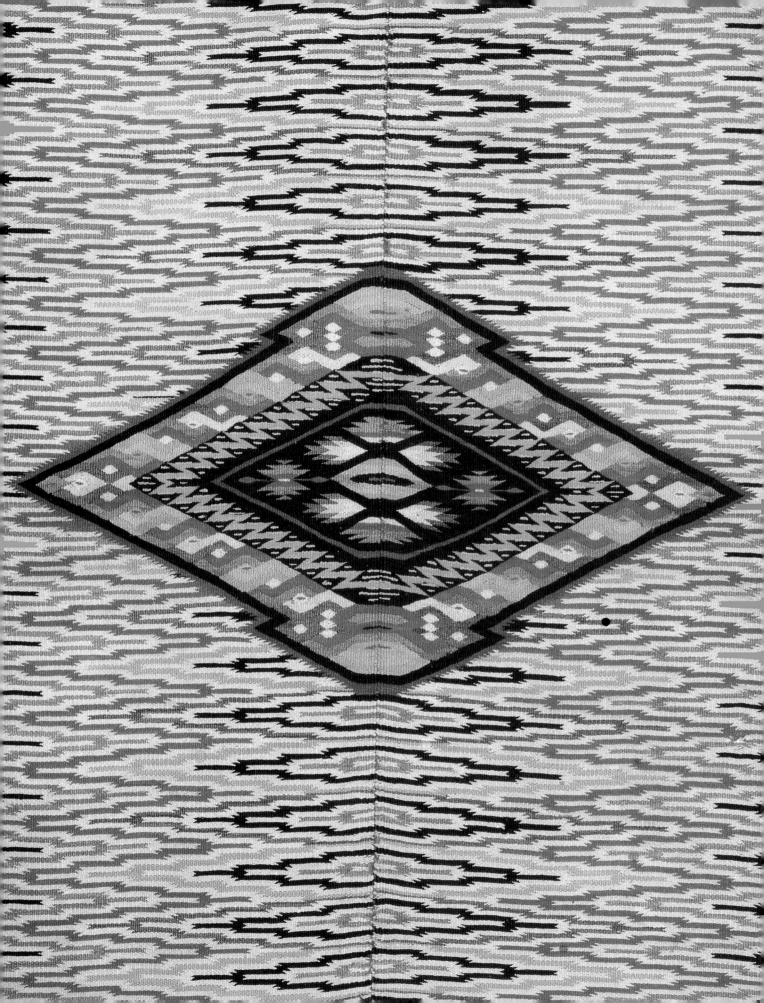

CHAPTER THREE
TEXTILES AND TRANSFORMATION

One of the most salient aspects of the Teotitlán textile industry is the flexibility and creativity with which weavers approach new market demands. Over the centuries they have had to be responsive to the shifting requirements of the masses. However, whether weaving for the Mixtec and Aztec empires, Spanish colonists, or North American importers, they have consistently produced highly respected and coveted textiles.

Following the introduction of wool and the fixed-frame pedal loom by the Spanish, the weaving industry underwent a series of transformations resulting in new manufacturing methods, color sources, and designs.

In the early years of the industry, Teotitlán weavers produced items of clothing such as wearing blankets, *sarapes*, and ponchos, for their own use and for trade with other Indians and the Spanish. Tightly woven, these early textiles were used as outer garments for protection from the elements.

As the market began to shift from native people to tourists, though, the function and style of the weavings also changed. Exposure to new ideas inspired tapestries patterned after famous paintings while a wave of national pride led to a celebration of ancient designs. Moreover, textiles now functioned as home decorations rather than clothing, art to be displayed rather than worn.

Then, with the advent of a cash economy weavers created another new textile form—the rug. Like the Navajos, whose patterns were developed collaboratively with reservation traders, the Teotitecos were influenced by U.S. importers. Together they developed new designs and colors that would be favored by American buyers. Still, the weavers never completely relinquished their heritage and also continued to produce tapestries and rugs that reflected their own history and culture.

During the 1800s, several major transformations occurred in the Mexican weaving industry: free labor replaced forced and indebted labor; large factories gave way to small workshops often owned and operated by Indian families; and control of the industry passed from the Spanish to the weavers themselves (Jeter and Juelke 1978: 22).

At this time, paintings and books depicting life in eighteenth- and nineteenth-century Mexico suddenly began to show weavings of riveting detail and unsurpassed refinement. Known as Saltillo *sarapes*, these weavings were shown cushioning a horseman's saddle or gracing the horseman himself. Saltillo *sarapes* are a distinctive art form that combines native and foreign patterns. At the high point of their production, they were so intricate and finely woven that only the very affluent were able to afford them. Later, as demand for them increased, weavers created simpler versions in order to produce greater quantities. By the Mexican War of Independence, in 1821, probably only less complex types of Saltillo *sarapes* were still being woven (Jeter and Juelke 1978: 24).

Known as "wearing blankets," *sarapes* were used by both native commoners and the Spanish elite, although the most exquisite ones were worn by Spanish upper-class men, *caballeros* who rode horseback to denote their status (Jeter and Juelke 1978: 7). Like the early Zapotec aristocracy, to signify their prestige in society the Spanish elite wore distinctive clothing made of silk, velvet, linen, and lace fabrics Indians were forbidden to wear.

While there were countless variations, typical design elements of the Saltillo *sarape* included a border; a background field incorporating elaborate repeating elements such as diagonal stripes, zigzags, or dots; and a central serrated diamond or circular medallion most often outlined in a color contrasting with its background. Each of these elements was made up of smaller motifs, such as triangles, ovals, and rhomboids (Jeter and Juelke 1978: 12). The overall effect was almost three-dimensional: a center design floating above a shimmering field encased within a frame. The fact that these complicated blankets were woven in two pieces and sewn together—thus requiring the weaver to perfectly match the halves—makes these creations even more impressive.

It is likely that yarns from churro or merino sheep were used to weave Saltillo *sarapes*. Spinners had to refine their technique, rendering very fine yarns to create the sharp angles in *sarape* designs. Because such intricate weavings required a strong warp yarn, this was presumably handspun. The colors were obtained from natural dyes, such as cochineal (red) and indigo (blue). *Sarapes* produced after the Mexican War were made using aniline dyes as well.

Though they emanate from the northern region of Saltillo, historical evidence suggests it was the Tlaxcalans from the south who first produced Saltillo *sarapes*, drawing on motifs devised by pre-Columbian ancestors (Jeter and Juelke 1978: 12). The round medallion found in the center of many of these *sarapes* possibly resulted from exposure to Oriental and European fabrics. Imported by Spain via Veracruz, Mexico, such fabrics were purchased by merchants, who distributed them throughout the country (Jeter and Juelke 1978: 14).

There is also some indication that other villages produced Saltillo-style *sarapes*, including Teotitlán. However, because the first documented *sarape* from Teotitlán dates back only to 1900, their early production in the village cannot be verified. Researchers continue to search for more clues about the history and evolution of these weavings, focusing on differences in wool, characteristics of spun yarn, and quality of threads in various types of *sarapes* (d'Avila 1998).

Some Mexican textile collectors believe that except for the wide band of horizontal stripes on the top and bottom and variations in the side borders, the dyes, colors, patterns, and weaving methods of what presumably are Teotitlán *sarapes* are identical to the characteristics of Saltillo *sarapes*, illustrating the degree to which Teotiteco weavers accommodated changing market demands (Winter 1998). In fact, according to village legend, up until the mid-1900s, Teotitlán was considered the premier blanket weaving center in southern Mexico, with creations traded as far as Chiapas and even in Guatemala. Modern weavers say their forebears made regular three-month religious pilgrimages by foot or burro to Esquipulas, a small town in Guatemala, trading their weavings along the way (Vásquez 1998).

Thus, throughout the eighteenth and nineteenth centuries, the Zapotec weavers made their living by farming and producing blankets, which were traded at both local and more distant markets, where they exchanged textiles for food staples such as maize and beans as well as weaving materials and dyes (Stephen 1991: 109).

Although the Mexican War of Independence ended in 1821 with the Treaty of Córdoba, proclaiming Mexico an independent nation (Miller 1985: 194), political unrest, which began in the 1800s, continued unabated for nearly a century. After a decade of war for independence, there followed wars with the United States and France; the confrontation between Indian President Benito Juárez and Austrian-born Emperor Maximilian; a long dictatorship under Porfirio Díaz; and the Mexican Revolution that put an end to debt peonage (Miller 1985).

During this time, Zapotec weavers lived in poverty due to prolonged national strife. It appears they continued to create two-piece simplified *sarapes*, though some intricate designs were produced. Using undyed fleece or bright aniline colors, they generally wove designs encompassing large central medallions (for example, the *sol de Oaxaca* and the Zapotec *estrella*) or mythic figures, both of which were set against a plain, striped, or dotted field, with broad bands of color either on the top and bottom of the weaving or stopping just short of the central design.

An enduring pattern, "El Diamante," or Zapatec Sun, continues to be woven today as it was in this cochineal-dyed *sarape* from 1900. Photo by A.L. Richardson. Courtesy of the Maxwell Museum, University of New Mexico.

From 1910 to 1920, almost a million people lost their lives to the Great Revolution, a confusing series of civil wars, conspiracies, and changing coalitions of rebel leaders. With the ascension of Alvaro Obregón to the office of president, a period of postwar reconstruction ensued (Miller 1985: 309). Aware of continuing discontent among peasants who had lost their land, President Obregón redistributed almost two and a half million acres to the Indian populace and granted titles to those who had taken back their land by force. Moreover, his minister of education ordered the construction of more than a thousand rural schools and hundreds of libraries in addition to training teachers, public health workers, and agricultural specialists (Miller 1985: 310).

Perhaps most significant for Teotitlán, the education minister supported the arts, including folk art and traditional music. This period resulted in a surge of civic pride and a glorification of Indians and pre-Columbian traditions. The government also encouraged Indian groups to preserve and develop their own ethnic identities (Miller 1985: 310). Time-honored foods, costumes, and crafts attained the status of national treasures.

This change in the political landscape, along with the completion of the Pan-American Highway in 1948 under President Lázaro Cárdenas, gave rise to increasing tourism (Miller 1985: 322). Vacationing Mexicans and other travelers now had easier access to Oaxaca's crafts markets. Zapotec weavers were quick to take advantage of their renewed popularity, reviving ancient patterns and rendering them in novel combinations and colors. Typical designs from this era are the *caracol* (snail), stepped fret, and other interlocking geometric patterns found on ancient ruins, notably the Mixtec necropolis of Mitla. Still other weavers interpreted Zapotec, Mayan, and Aztec mythological figures or employed stylized animal and flower motifs taken from pre-Columbian clay stamps. One of the first weavers to do this, Isaac Vásquez, created a portfolio of such images that are still used by the villagers.

With tourism came exposure to new ideas and designs, which the versatile Teotitecos incorporated into their repertoire. But only the most experienced weavers, ones who had mastered the difficult art of weaving curvilinear lines, could create the newest type of weavings—tapestries modeled after famous paintings by artists such as Pablo Picasso, Paul Klee, Henri Matisse, M. C. Escher, and Mexico's Diego Rivera.

Despite interest in their textiles, Teotitlán's weavers still struggled financially, most barely supporting themselves with weavings and subsistence farming. Their pre-colonial system of reciprocal exchange of goods, known as *guelaguetza*, surely helped the town survive. Under this system, villagers borrowed goods from one another during times of hardship or for important occasions—such as when chickens and mescal were needed for a wedding (Stephen 1991: 194). The lending party kept a tally of what was owed and could request repayment when it was deemed necessary. In this way, Teotitecos have been able to help one another during times of need, and a version of this system continues to the present day.

From the 1920s to the 1940s, the economic situation of Teotitlán's citizens further deteriorated when automated textile factories in large Mexican cities diversified and produced cotton and wool fabrics in great quantity. With access to cheaper factory-made blankets, the country looked to other sources of practical woolen goods (Stephen 1991: 120).

To help alleviate economic hardship, in the 1940s the governments of Mexico and the United States joined forces to resurrect the *bracero* (hired hand) program, whereby Mexicans could migrate to North America, work the agricultural fields, and return home with cash. Workers received guaranteed round-trip transportation, fair wages, and adequate housing. This arrangement both aided U.S. farmers, who needed extra employees during World War II, and also helped the Mexican government relieve the poverty of indigenous populations, which had plagued them since the Spanish conquest (Stephen 1991: 111).

Although this program ended for the most part by 1950, it forever changed the economy and worldview of Teotitlán's weavers in several ways. First, after returning to Teotitlán many weavers created their own businesses, some even hiring other locals and even weavers from neighboring villages. Moreover, the program sparked interest in working abroad in the United States, and many weavers, sometimes with their families, went there independent of government programs. One of these weavers ultimately transformed the Teotitlán textile industry. While working in the 1960s as a taxi driver in Texas, Ismael Gutiérrez noticed woven textiles used on floors instead of as blankets or ponchos and upon his return to Teotitlán "invented" rugs (Roth 1998). Previously, Teotitlán weavers had marketed their textiles only as blankets or tapestries, having no notion of the existence of rugs when tourists or U.S. buyers had requested them. However, after Gutiérrez introduced the concept of the rug a revolution occurred in Teotitlán textiles, that eventually resulted in the economic and creative development of the industry.

Plate 11
Unknown weaver,
c. early to
mid-19th century
Untitled
52 x 92 ins.

From Teotitlán del Valle,
this traditional *sarape*
design is composed of
many shades of vegetal
dyes, including three
shades of blue and one
shade of green from
indigo; three shades of
red most probably from
cochineal; and yellow,
gold, and pink from other
organic sources. It was
woven in two pieces.
Weaving courtesy of
Mark and Lerin Winter,
Santa Fe, NM.

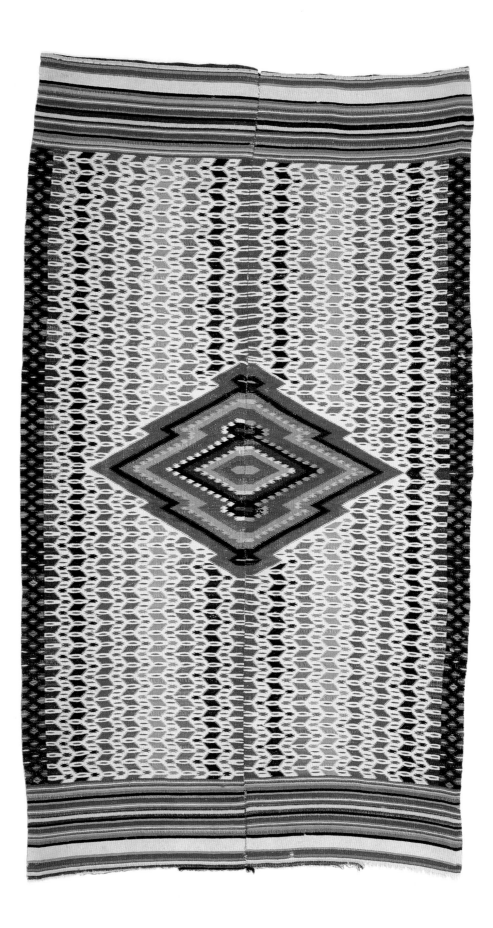

Plate 12
Unknown weaver,
c. early to
mid-19th century
Untitled
47 x 86 ins.

This traditional Teotitlán del Valle *sarape* design, comprised of two pieces, embodies numerous shades of blue from indigo and gold dye derived from vegetal sources. The brown is undyed fleece. Weaving courtesy of Mark and Lerin Winter, Santa Fe, NM.

Plate 13
Unknown weaver,
c. late 19th century
Untitled
48 x 79 ins.

From Teotitlán del Valle,
this *sarape* design reflects
a color palette created
with both aniline and natural dyes. Woven in two
pieces. Weaving courtesy
of Mark and Lerin Winter,
Santa Fe, NM.

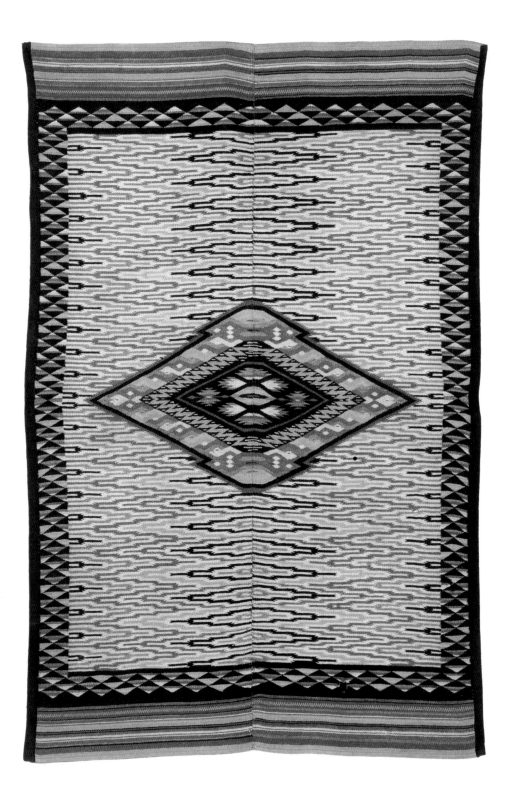

Plate 14
Unknown weaver,
c. late 19th century
Untitled
53 x 78 ins.

Another Oaxaca-made *sarape*, this design is made up of a circular medallion with an outer wreath. There is a foreshortened spot-repeat field on a white background, spot-repeat side borders, and banded and patterned ends. This particular pattern differs from typical Saltillo *sarapes*, which have a border on all four sides and typically no bands of color on either end. Weaving courtesy of Mark and Lerin Winter, Santa Fe, NM.

Plate 15
Unknown weaver,
c. 1930s
Estrella de Oaxaca
(Star of Oaxaca)
62 x 81 ins.

This is a traditional *sarape*
design of undyed fleece
woven in two pieces. Both
the warp and the weft
were handspun. Weaving
courtesy of Scott Roth.

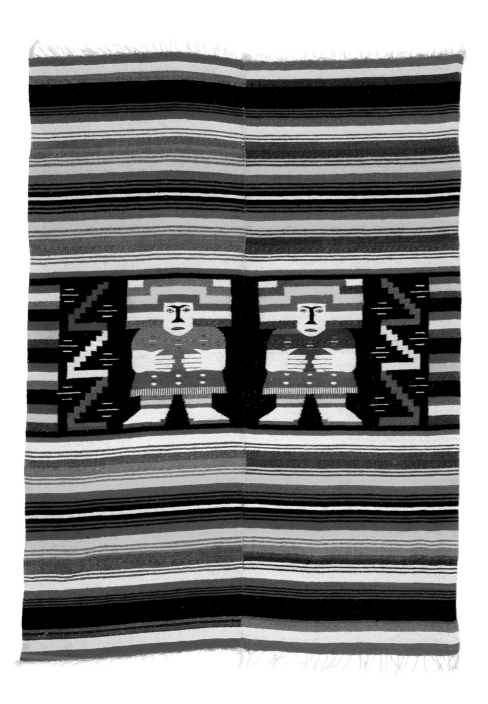

Plate 16
Unknown weaver,
c. 1930s
Untitled
55 x 75 ins.

This is a traditional *sarape* design of handspun warp and weft yarns. The aniline dyes, popular during this era, account for the bright colors. This two-piece textile is a type often referred to as a *cobija matrimonio*, or matrimonial blanket. Weaving courtesy of Scott Roth.

Plate 17
Erasto Gutiérrez, 1996
Untitled
40 x 47 ins.

This is an interpretation of Pablo Picasso's *Woman at a Window* (1936). Aniline dyes and handspun yarns were used. Weaving courtesy of Scott Roth.

Plate 18
Ricardo Martínez, 1984
Untitled
37 x 55 ins.

This weaving is an adaptation of M. C. Escher's *Sky and Water 11* (1938). Escher was inspired by the interlocking mirror-image geometric patterns carved in the stone facades of ancient Mitla in the Oaxaca Valley. His designs later became favorites of Teotitlán weavers. The dyes are aniline, and the yarn is handspun. Weaving courtesy of Scott Roth.

Plate 19
The Family of Lasero
Montaño, 1978
Greca Victoriano
(Victoriano's Zapotec
Geometric)
57 x 75 ins.

Created in the 1930s by
the weaver Victoriano,
it was a popular *sarape*
pattern among Teotitecos.
Weaving courtesy of
Scott Roth.

Plate 20
Unknown Weaver,
c. 1930s
Untitled
58 x 76 ins.

This piece represents the Aztec calendar, a traditional *sarape* design. The red, white, and green bands of the Mexican flag reflect the nationalistic pride that swept the country after the Revolution of 1910. The handspun yarn is synthetically dyed. Weaving courtesy of Scott Roth.

CHAPTER FOUR
THE U.S. CONNECTION: RECENT RUG PRODUCTION

By the 1970s carpenters in Teotitlán were constructing larger looms to accommodate the weavers' latest product—rugs. Initially, looms only yielded four-foot-wide weavings, but it was not long before they produced ten- and twelve-foot ones. Now the stage was set for an entirely new phase of textile production.

In 1974, the publication of an issue of *Arizona Highways* devoted to the finest contemporary Navajo rugs sparked an explosion of interpretive and imitative weaving by Teotitlán weavers (Roth 1998). They again saw an opportunity to attract a unique customer—this time the North American homeowner. With the help of importers from the United States, who first introduced Navajo designs to the Zapotec Indians, their aspirations were realized. Today, all weavers in the village dream of finding an importer who will buy their rugs and sell them in the United States. Though once the majority of weavings were sold to tourists or Mexican nationals, in the 1970s the market shifted as the peso lost value and the purchasing power of the U.S. dollar rose dramatically. Now weaving production in Teotitlán focused on an export market, and importers became a powerful voice in determining color schemes, designs, and overall rug quality.

The importers soon devised methods to work with weaving families and get their products out of Mexico. The Zapotec Indians were perfectly suited to weaving for this new market: a talented and motivated source of labor with a high degree of technical expertise and accustomed to satisfying other peoples' tastes.

Each importer had a personal view of what would sell and how to work with the weavers. Some even imagined themselves to be in the position of the white traders who had worked with the Navajos, such as Lorenzo Hubbell and J. B. Moore. Indeed, in many respects the development of the Zapotec rug industry closely resembles the history of Navajo weaving.

For both the Zapotec and the Navajos the first consumers of weavings were their own people or other Indians; both wove for a secular market rather than making weavings for ceremonial use, thereby creating designs that could be adapted to the style of the day (Rodee 1995); and both eventually began weaving for a wider export market.

After being released from internment at Bosque Redondo (Fort Sumner), where they had been exposed to new weaving designs and methods, the Navajos were settled onto reservation lands in Arizona. With the coming of the railroad, their isolation ended, and traders and travelers sought out their wares (Rodee 1995). These events roughly correspond to the construction of the Pan-American Highway in Mexico, which brought the Zapotec weavers into the national arena.

Then at the urging of traders, Navajo weavers gradually transformed their thin, tightly woven blankets into heavier, thicker rugs. To accommodate the tastes of buyers in the East, many new designs were introduced, especially those found in Oriental carpets. Some traders created new designs while others sought to preserve or revive older patterns. Like the importers working with the Zapotec, the New Mexico traders' influence was intended to improve the quality of the weavers' rugs and make them more marketable.

For Zapotec and Navajo weavers alike, such influence had both advantages and disadvantages. While both peoples owe economic success to the designs proffered by outsiders, they also have had to squelch desires to develop more personal work related to their own lives and cultures. Today, tired of a decade of foreign influence, many Zapotec weavers are exploring other sources of inspiration.

Richard Enzer chose to work with the Zapotec weavers of Teotitlán because he recognized, "No other weavers are as talented as the Zapotecs when it comes to flat-weave rugs. No one else knows how to use the horizontal loom as they do. They are open to any design, any technique. They've always had to weave for others—the Zapotec aristocracy, the Aztecs, the Spanish—and they are up to the challenge."

In 1982, Enzer began creating a new collection of rugs he calls Line of the Spirit, which celebrates the interconnectedness of all peoples around the globe. He taught himself the intricacies of dyeing wool and, with help from Pedro Gutiérrez, an expert dyer, perfected the look of "abrash," or subtle color gradation, in the backgrounds of his designs. This almost imperceptible striping gives the rugs a rich tonality, the look of antiques. Enzer explains that nomadic weavers in the Middle East collected plants for dyes as they traveled; each batch would yield a "dye lot" so that when a rug was woven, many shades of one color could be combined to produce depth and movement. Enzer says, "I use color as design and tonality as a design element. There is texture to the color in these rugs."

For his collection, intended to incorporate motifs from many cultures, he and his design assistant, Sergio Martínez, introduced symbolic "floating elements"—small colorful shapes against a tonal background. Connected to no other part of the rugs' designs, they seem to drift in space. These symbols, which Enzer calls "spirit messengers," "gods' eyes," "butterfly wings," "rattlesnake tails," and so on, represent such concepts as harmony, good harvest, bravery, introspection, and luck.

Years after Enzer first introduced his line of rugs, his ideas are still reflected in most of the weavings being made in Teotitlán today, some of which are illustrated in prestigious magazines such as *Architectural Digest*.

Many weavers express mixed feelings when they speak about Enzer. Some feel grateful that he helped open up U.S. markets to them by creating attractive and popular designs. He also gave work to the many weavers who produced his rugs, including their names on all of his price tags. Yet others see him as an outsider who disrupted the delicate kinship and community relationships by which the people of Teotitlán conduct their businesses and lives.

Enzer has his own ambivalent feelings about the impact that relative prosperity has had on Teotitlán's textile industry. Comparing Teotitlán's character upon his arrival with later changes, he says: "It was a sleepy village and very primitive. But the people were steeped in their culture. Age and experience earned them status and respect. It all made sense. With the success of their rug sales in the 1980s, they suddenly had money. We think we help people by helping them to make money, but money changes people, and it changes systems. The pecking order changes—the more affluent become the leaders instead of those with wisdom. I saw alcoholism and materialism develop. People began to buy things that didn't make sense—color TVs and CD players—while they still lacked bathrooms, clean water, and things that really would make their lives easier."

Enzer's newest project is teaching his designs to fifty weavers in eastern Europe, where he chose to resettle because his ancestors originated there, coming from a town a stone's throw away from his present workshop. Says Enzer, "I liked working with the Zapotecs, but I needed to find my own tribe. It's very exciting to find my own roots. It deepens my understanding of the Indians in Teotitlán, and the sense of identity they get from being part of a community that they can trace back through time to its earliest beginnings. It gives an individual a sense of belonging, and a sense of place."

One of the first North American buyers to come to Teotitlán, Jane Kelly in the early days had no easy way to get her precious finds out of the area and back to her hometown. To circumvent obstacles, she had to bribe officials with perfume and cigarettes and make special trips to Mexico City because the government's square export stamp had been replaced with a round stamp. Kelly credits Anastacio Gutiérrez, son of a prominent weaver in town, for helping her devise ways to export her purchases. In fact, he had a unique position in the village, made necessary because of the new markets opening up in the United States.

She continues to visit Teotitlán four times a year for several weeks at a time, staying with the Montaño family, who in addition to weaving owns one of the three restaurants in town as well as a two-story shop with a winding staircase and shady courtyard. Says Kelly, "When I first came to Teotitlán, I made business deals on dirt floors by candlelight or a single bare bulb. Now that they are successful, you see the weavers putting their earnings into their homes, or a truck, or better looms, more wool. It doesn't make sense to put their money in a bank because the peso is always being devalued. What I really respect about them is that everyone attends fiestas—the most affluent, the least affluent, and everyone in between. You have to be humble here, you can't lord your success over others. It's not good manners."

Kelly fondly recalls the many fiestas in which she has participated and describes the town's New Year's Day ritual and how it has been somewhat altered by modernity: "All the villagers walk up into the mountains and make wishes for the coming year. They collect stones there in the mountains, and with them build a miniature house. Having a house might be part of their wish, but they also wish for such things as chickens, a pig, a car, children, more money. Afterwards they pay homage to the Virgin Mary and have a barbecue. In the old days, everybody used to walk up, but now everyone drives, and it's like a parking lot up there."

In addition to admiring the fiestas, Kelly appreciates the way Teotitecos are able to keep their culture intact in the face of so much pressure from the modern world: "Weavers fold up the day's work for family or community or religious events. I love that about them. It's not the most efficient way to run a business, but it means that their business lives don't consume them the way work consumes so many people here in the States."

Though he admires many of Teotitlán's talented weavers, importer Scott Roth is partial to Isaac Vásquez. Says Roth, "As early as the 1960s Isaac was a leader. He was not a wealthy man, and like many others, he had to weave to support himself and his family. He was extremely innovative. While in his twenties, he researched how to use vegetal dyes, and he began using them in his work. He developed formulas for cochineal, rock lichen, indigo, and huizache. He also expanded the designs the town used by creating tapestries from famous paintings. And he experimented with pre-Columbian motifs,

especially Indian deities. His work has always been beautifully interpretive with much life and animation to it. There's no question about it, he was a major influence in creating the new tourist market."

Roth remembers Isaac Vásquez as the individual who made him aware that many of the weavers, in the early days, were using factory-made yarns with a high percentage of acrylic fibers, saying, "He showed me how the fibers of the rugs were shiny in the sun, a sure sign of synthetic yarn. He also taught me about 'fugitive dyes'—dyes that had not been properly set and were not colorfast. It took a while for the weavers to understand the importance of good quality fibers and dyes, and Isaac has certainly been at the vanguard of that campaign."

Another important lesson learned from Vásquez was the extraordinary degree of skill required to weave curvilinear forms. Many Zapotec weavings depict birds, bears, deer, and other animals with rounded shapes. Says Roth, "Isaac explained to me that a good weaver does not 'staircase' his stitches, that is, he forms a smooth edge instead of a jagged one. This is very hard to accomplish. It takes a weaver an average of five years to learn to make a seamless, flowing curved line. Isaac is, of course, an expert at it."

When visiting Teotitlán three months each year, Roth stays at the home of Januario González and Macaria Ruiz, where he has his own room decorated with some of his favorite rugs. In the family's altar room, stacks of beautifully rendered weavings embody some of Roth's own ideas to improve the industry. For example, he supplies the weavers with whom he works with a thicker four-ply instead of the standard two-

Januario Gonzalez sketches a new design of interlocking fish. Most of the weavers in Teotitlán who use curvilinear forms first prepare a full-size drawing, which they place underneath the warp threads and refer to during the weaving process.

ply wool for the foundation threads, making the rugs heavier and more likely to lie flat. Roth has also developed an original way to finish the rugs: He has the weavers sew the fringes back into the body of the rug, then secure a woven wool braid to protect the vulnerable edges.

Though he was given the opportunity to stay with other families in Teotitlán, Roth chose to live with González because of that weaver's dyeing expertise. Says Roth, "He learned dyeing with his brother-in-law, Emiliano Mendoza, who was one of the first great tapestry weavers in the village. Januario makes some of the richest, finest colors that exist in the village. He develops a new palette every few years. But, also, he is very generous with his wealth of experience. He is respected in town for his leadership abilities. He gives good counsel and has served on many committees, including the committee that designed Teotitlán's museum. I wanted to live with Januario because I recognized a genius, and I wanted to be close to him."

Of the many importers of Teotiteco rugs, Roth has, perhaps, focused the most intently on the history of the village. He has researched the subject in books and peri-

odicals and can recite dates of important community events, such as when the first piped water system was installed and celebrated. He himself organized a foot race up the mountains, which he plans to hold annually, with commemorative T-shirts for everyone at the finish line. The race, in a way, serves as a metaphor for the friendly but vigorous competition that exists in Teotitlán on a daily basis. No matter who wins the race, everyone benefits from the town's vitality and success.

Macaria Ruiz and Elena Gonzalez finish a large rug by weaving a braided cord onto each end.

Plate 21
Felix Gonzales, 1990
Nomadic Design
69 x 96 ins.

An original composition by
importer Richard Enzer for
his "Line of the Spirit"
tapestry collection.
Weaving courtesy of
Richard Enzer.

Plate 22
Mito Martínez, 1986
Diamonds in the Sky
65 x 92 ins.

This original design by
Richard Enzer represents
the spiritual unity of all
peoples. It is of aniline
dyes and handspun wool
from Chichicapa. Weaving
courtesy of Richard Enzer.

Plate 23
Felipe Hernández, 1998
Hearst #235,
or **Doble Cadena**
(Double Chain)
48 x 72 ins.

This Navajo blanket pattern was introduced to Teotitecos by U.S. importers in the 1980s. Today it is commonly woven in many color combinations. This example is of aniline dyes and handspun yarn.

Plate 24
Juan Luis, 1991
Manuelito
65 x 91 ins.

An original design by
Richard Enzer. It is of aniline dyes and handspun
wool from Chichicapa.

Plate 25
Juvenal Mendoza, 1997
Untitled
24 x 36 ins.

This is a signed original
composition using Navajo
motifs and serrated dia-
monds, finely woven and
dramatic against a dark
background.

Plate 26
Manuel Montaño, 1998
Two Grey Hills
78 x 120 ins.

This design is adapted
from a contemporary
Navajo pattern, although
its vibrant colors, from
aniline dyes, give it a
distinctly Zapotec flavor.
Weaving courtesy of
Scott Roth.

Plate 27
Isaac Vásquez, 1992
Untitled
43 x 53 ins.

Vásquez's original composition, woven by his son Geronimo Vásquez, is adapted from a pre-Columbian clay stamp of a double-headed bird found at Calixtahuaca. Made of yarn spun on a spinning wheel and natural and aniline dyes. Weaving courtesy of Scott Roth.

Plate 28
Antonio Martínez, 1998
Jaguar y Serpiente
(Jaguar and Serpent)
34 x 71 ins.

An original, signed composition taken from a pre-Columbian clay stamp found at Veracruz. Natural dyes and handspun yarn were used.

Plate 29
Felipe Hernández, 1997
Hearst #156
48 x 72 ins.

This is a Navajo blanket
pattern adapted from a
weaving in the William
Randolph Hearst
Collection, introduced to
the weavers by U. S.
importers. The dyes are
aniline, and the yarn was
handspun in Chichicapa.

Plate 30
Luis Bazan, 1997
Llaves Grandes
(Large Greek Keys)
48 x 72 ins.

An original design by
Richard Enzer utilizing
aniline dyes.

Plate 31
Isaac Vásquez, 1989
Untitled
42 x 57 ins.

This signed weaving is
an interpretation of a
four-inch disk with a
Mayan carving of a mon-
key. The colors are from
natural dyes while the
yarn was spun with both
a spinning wheel and a
drop-spindle. Weaving
courtesy of Scott Roth.

Plate 32
Bulmaro Pérez, 1998
Montanitas
(Little Mountains)
24 x 40 ins.

This weaving exemplifies
the weaver's rich, earthy
palette. The colors are
made from complicated
blends of aniline dyes.

CHAPTER FIVE
WOOL PROCESSING: PAST AND PRESENT

The village of Chichicapa, located in the Sierra Madre del Sur Mountains, is an important center for wool processing. The two-and-a-half-hour drive to the town over unpaved, rocky roads is slow and laborious. More than half of Mexico's inhabitants still live in rural areas like Chichicapa. Although each year highways connect more of the country, even today some regions have not yet been mapped, and many communities that are located no more than a few miles apart are cut off from each other by virtually impassable terrain. Because of such isolation, the villagers of Chichicapa see no more than a handful of foreigners in their lifetime, and their dialect of Zapotec confounds many Teotitecos, who also speak that language.

Wool used for Chichicapa's yarns comes from *Estante* (stationary), or churro, sheep, first introduced to Mexico by the Spanish. Because churro sheep were well suited to sparse, lowland country and tolerated poorer-quality vegetation, the Spanish brought herds of this breed to the New World for both meat and wool (Rodee 1995: 24). Churro wool was moderately coarse with long, straight, shiny wool fibers and a natural waxiness, or lanolin, that gave it a smooth, buttery feel (Gelenter 1998). Early in the Spanish colonial period, attempts were also made to introduce another breed of sheep, the merino (Jeter and Juelke 1978: 19). Native to Iraq, in the eighth century this breed was brought by the Moors to Spain, where it was improved through crossbreed-ing with British long-wool sheep. So highly regarded were these sheep that stealing even one from the royal families and clergy who owned them meant certain death. With fine, short, crimpy fibers, merino fleece was preferred for apparel, making clothing that conformed to the body and felt silky against the skin.

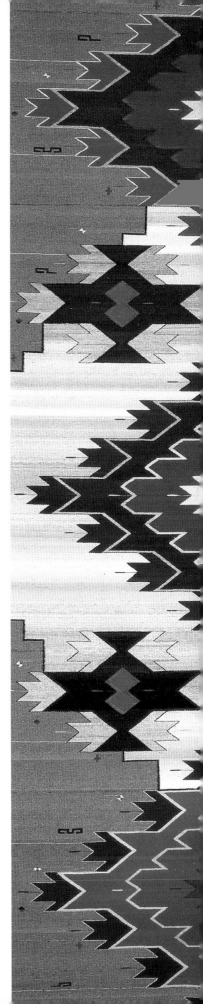

previous spread: Located high in the mountains of Oaxaca, Chichicapa is home to women spinners who produce beautiful yarn using the ancient drop-spindle. A wooden dowel tapered at both ends, the spindle is set into motion between the spinner's palms. As it rotates, one cylinder of wool after another is attached, forming a tight thread. The wool's natural twistiness lends a distinctive nubby texture.

However, this breed failed to take hold in Mexico, probably because it was introduced in limited quantities. In addition, merino wool required much more preparation than churro wool since another of its characteristics was its high grease content. To remove it, the wool first had to be thoroughly washed with strong solvents then rinsed with warm water so that residual grease did not remain trapped in the natural twist of the fiber. Water supplies for this process were probably inadequate. Further, locals might have considered it too labor-intensive as compared with the relatively limited processing needed for churro wool (Winter 1998).

Another drawback of merino wool was that because of the refinement it required, much of it was lost during processing. Only 60 percent of merino wool, by weight, remained after grease and damaged tips were removed while 90 percent of churro wool, by weight, was available after preparation. Moreover, due to its attenuated fibers, merino wool was more difficult to spin, and thus churro wool was more advantageous for Mexican weavers with limited resources and elementary tools (Winter 1998).

The churro sheep of Mexico today are very different from the original Spanish breed. Their wool is dry with short fibers and an abundant amount of hollow, wiry kemp hairs that are difficult to dye. The inferior qualities of their wool probably developed as a result of the harsh climate, poor nutrition, and centuries of indiscriminate inbreeding. Left to their own devices, the original churros and generations after them interbred and so diminished the available genetic material from which nature might have chosen more pleasing traits (Gelenter 1998). Over the years breeders have tried to improve the quality of churro fleece by introducing rams of other breeds with long, straight, buttery hair, such as the Romney and Lincoln, from Australia and New Zealand, to the herds. Because no systematic breeding programs were followed, though, the churro sheep again regressed to what is their present state of desiccation (Gelenter 1998).

Sabinas Pérez and Alicia Hernández sit on palm mats in the shade of a woven straw canopy, which offers some relief from the ninety-degree heat in this dusty town. The two friends enjoy conversation as they card and spin baskets of raw wool purchased in various Indian village markets such as Nochixtan, Tlacolula, and Ocotlán. Because their traditional homes lack windows and electricity for lights, they perform these tasks in the open air. Experience makes their work look effortless.

After thoroughly washing and drying her basket of wool, Hernández cards it by scraping handfuls against wooden panels shaped like Ping-Pong paddles, which have metal teeth on one side. She drags the first paddle's teeth over the wool resting on the second paddle's teeth, thus separating, stretching, straightening, and softening the fibers in preparation for spinning.

Next she rolls the scraped wool off the paddles into the shape of loose cylinders while Pérez deftly spins the wool into yarn, using an ancient drop-spindle, a tapered wooden dowel weighted at one end with a shallow ceramic cone, or whorl, and primed with a piece of yarn. She positions one end on the concave surface of a bowl resting on a cloth turban and sets the dowel into motion between her palms. As it rotates at a good clip, Pérez attaches one cylinder of wool after another to the forming yarn, adjusting the tension carefully to maintain a uniform thickness throughout the skein.

Alternately, it is also possible to spin yarn using a spinning wheel, a machine first introduced by the Spanish and used in other pueblos today, including Teotitlán, where villagers produce yarn for their own use or for sale. A spinning wheel is operated by a crank, which sets a large vertical wheel into motion, causing a horizontally positioned spindle to rotate. The spinner turns the crank with one hand and attaches cylinders of carded wool to a primed spindle with the other.

In another area of Chichicapa, another Zapotec woman graciously offers mescal while she spills hampers of wool balls on the floor, initiating the bargaining process. In setting prices, the townspeople compete primarily with modern wool factories, such as

Balls of undyed handspun yarn from Chichicapa rest at the feet of Zacarias Soza and his mother, Delfina Mendoza. Churro sheep produce a surprising range of colored wool, from blue-grays and golden yellows to dark browns and creamy whites. The interlocking diamond pattern of Soza's rug has a decidedly modern feel. His natural dyes include shades of blue from indigo and red from the larvae of the cochineal insect.

Introduced by the Spanish, the spinning wheel is used in many communities, especially Teotitlán, where villagers produce yarn for sale or for family use. A hand crank sets the large vertical wheel in motion causing a horizontally positioned spindle to rotate. Delfina Mendoza turns the crank with one hand while she attaches cylinders of carded wool with the other.

those in Tlaxcala and Toluca, where huge carding machines separate and straighten fleece and spin it using seventy-five-foot devices with hundreds of metal spindles.

Teotitlán's own wool factory, opened in 1983 amid controversy, was funded by federal and state agencies to provide weavers with locally produced, high-quality yarn at low prices. However, since it is state-operated, Teotitecos have never considered it

their own and have even objected to its
name, La Lanera de Oaxaca (the Wool
Factory of Oaxaca), which they feel
should have been named after Teotitlán
(Stephen 1991: 142). Fortunately, after
the factory nearly went bankrupt, the
state allowed a town committee to manage it, making it more acceptable to the
people.

Now Teotiteco weavers see positive
aspects of the factory. They appreciate
the fact that it produces needed varie-
gated light gray yarns that can be
overdyed successfully, yielding a tonal

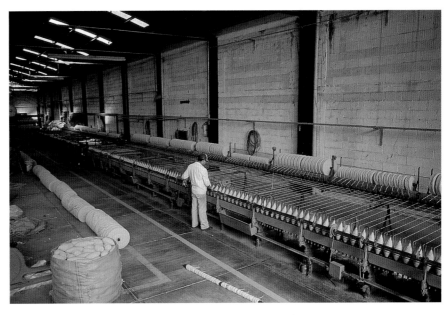

Opened in 1983,
Teotitlán's wool factory
spins raw wool into yarn
using mechanical spinners.
The town's weavers appre-
ciate the fact that this factory refuses to incorporate
acrylic fibers into its skeins
as other factories some-
times do.

field. Also, residents can be confident about the wool's purity because the factory
refuses to incorporate acrylic fibers into yarns as other factories sometimes do.
Moreover, it is convenient to have large quantities of yarn locally available, considering
the fact that an average six-foot by nine-foot rug requires fifteen pounds of wool.

Despite the convenience of factory wool, handspun wool is considered superior
because it retains a nubby texture, has greater strength, and is more resistant to dam-
age. Since the yarn undergoes minimal processing, handcarding and handspinning
result in the greater retention of natural lanolin as well. While this substance makes the
rugs moisture- and soil-repellent, it also makes the wool more difficult to dye evenly.
For that reason, weavers often use factory wool if a design calls for large areas of a single
color. Still, for the most beautiful wool, Teotitecos come to Chichicapa and to other
remote towns, where ancient processing traditions continue to hold sway.

Plate 33
Eligio Bazan, 1998
Multi-Texcoco
120 x 180 ins.

An original composition, this design is patterned after a *sarape* from Texcoco, Mexico. It is a fine example of the weaver's use of natural dyes, with five shades of indigo and eight shades of cochineal. Weaving courtesy of Scott Roth.

Plate 34
Zacarias Soza, 1996
Mil Estrellas
(A Thousand Stars)
48 x 78 ins.

This original composition uses rare tones of undyed churro wool fleece as well as cochineal, indigo, and *vejugo* (yellow derived from tree lichen) dyes. The warp and weft yarns were handspun. Weaving courtesy of Scott Roth.

Plate 35
Alberto Vásquez, 1995
La Tierra (The Earth)
32 x 60 ins.

An original composition
made with natural dyes of
lichen, cochineal, and
indigo. Weaving courtesy
of Scott Roth.

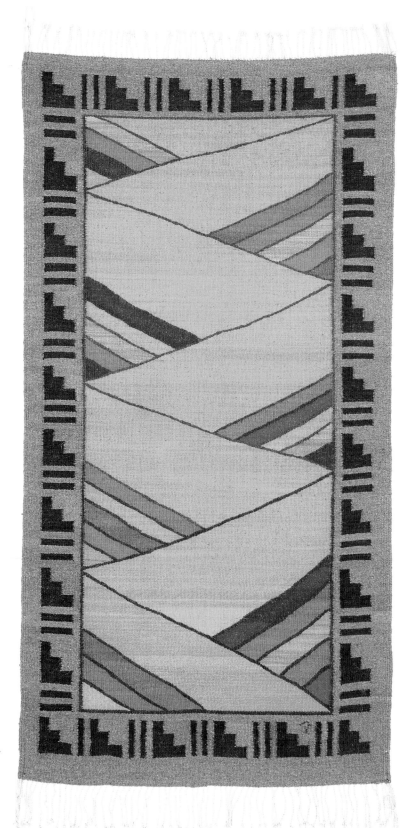

Plate 36
Isaac Vásquez, n.d.
Untitled
39 x 50 ins.

This signed composition is adapted from a cave painting in France that the weaver saw in a book. The light shades were obtained by using a second dye bath. The yellow dye is derived from rock moss and the red from cochineal. The yarn was spun with a spinning wheel. Weaving courtesy of Scott Roth.

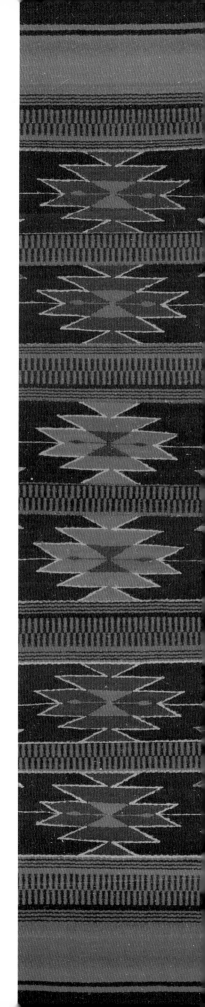

CHAPTER SIX
QUALITIES OF
ZAPOTEC TEXTILES

Because of their undeniable charm and the dedication they exhibit to their craft, it is easy to romanticize the Zapotec weavers of Teotitlán. Their simple attire, gracious manner, affinity with nature, and identification with their community all contribute to their appeal. This seems especially true for North Americans, whose lives often seem impossibly complicated and impersonal.

In this era of megastores, malls, and electronic chat rooms, is it any wonder that we are attracted to a people who seem to have a simpler existence and to embody qualities we yearn for in ourselves and in our neighbors—loyalty, consideration, compassion, and mutual respect?

However, while Teotitecos undoubtedly possess an unusual degree of conviviality, their lives differ little from the lives of others in a small-town environment anywhere in the world. In fact, in some ways the pressures of their small-town existence are magnified due to the fact that almost everyone pursues the same occupation. Inevitably some weavers are more fortunate, talented, or perspicacious than others, a result of the uneven distribution of natural ability, societal support, and luck in any group of people. Consequently, some Teotitlán families have beautiful brick homes with Spanish-style iron scrollwork while others live in modest clay or brick structures with dirt floors.

Moreover, despite considerable community cooperation and the fact that the Zapotecs consider envy evil, competitiveness and subtle forms of sabotage certainly exist in Teotitlán. For example, one weaver might feign ignorance when asked for directions to a second weaver's display booth in a small crafts market, even when the second weaver's booth is only around the corner. Similarly, weavers sometimes downplay their

The weekly market in Tlacolula.

competitor's abilities or imply that their neighbors are unscrupulous in some way, such as about information given concerning the quality or nature of their dyes.

Despite the people's humility, they exhibit pride as well. Though weavers rarely claim to be the best textile maker in town, some develop a kind of conceit. For instance, one of the more famous weavers wanted to charge a customer five times what other weavers charge for a rug with a common, relatively simple design. When the customer protested, the weaver stood firm and was content to let the customer leave his showroom without having made a purchase. This is ironic given that less affluent weavers living nearby are often desperate to make a sale.

Such gaps in business practices arise from the fact that while the people of Teotitlán are among the most prosperous of Mexico's Indian populations, many are terribly poor by U.S. standards. It is therefore understandable that some weavers occasionally misrepresent aspects of their weavings, such as claiming they use natural dyes when their colors are actually obtained with synthetic dyes, in order to attract tourists who they believe have a higher regard for traditional dye methods. If it means the difference between selling a rug or going hungry, they may embellish the truth—as most people would behave under the circumstances. In truth, it can be argued that synthetic dyes are not intrinsically inferior to vegetable dyes. The use of each demands extensive knowledge and experience. Because corrosive ingredients such as sulfuric acid are required to make synthetic dyes permanent, they can be extremely dangerous to work with. In one instance, unaware of the necessity of keeping the dye bath cool when adding acid, a weaver almost went blind when the bath exploded in his face.

Buyers of Teotitlán textiles must select from a wide range of styles and colors and must assess numerous qualities. Though only a fraction of the village's weavers produce exceptional weavings in terms of a uniquely imaginative use of colors, designs, or methods, hundreds of others create beautiful, playful, elegant, or interesting textiles. In Teotitlán, there is a weaving to suit every person's taste.

When choosing weavings it is helpful to know the characteristics of a well-made piece, especially if the weaving is to be used on the floor. For example, a loosely woven rug will be floppy and limp in contrast to a more tightly woven one. In addition, rugs that have visible white warp threads or puckered rather than straight edges are not desirable. With larger rugs, an exceptionally sturdy one will have a double warp. An easy way to ascertain this information is to observe the warp threads as they emerge from either end of the weaving and begin to form the fringe. If a double warp was used, two white threads can be seen, but in the case of a single warp, only one.

If the weaving is to be used as a rug, it is also a good idea to test the colorfastness of the dye since at some point the rug will need to be cleaned. To do this, rub the surface of the weaving with a dry piece of muslin or other light-colored cloth. If the dye does not transfer, there is a good chance the color is permanent. Rubbing the surface with a damp cloth would be an even better test, but some weavers might not allow this procedure. Some importers recommend buying a small panel from a weaver and testing it thoroughly with water. However, it would be essential to make certain that the small panel was dyed in the same way as the larger piece. Of course, if the weaving is to be used on the wall as a tapestry, such testing is less necessary.

Because a very small minority of weavers use fibers other than wool, it is a good idea to watch out for acrylic yarns. A method for identifying such yarns is to hold the weaving in the sunlight and look for shiny synthetic fibers. Still, if a weaving is compelling, there is no reason to pass it by regardless of whether or not it contains acrylic yarns.

The best weavings have a nubby, nonuniform yarn achieved through handspinning techniques. To identify handspun yarn, look for a bumpy, textured surface. (Beware of pilling that results from the use of the sheep's short down fibers, which work their way up to the surface of the weaving.) Or, if a spare piece of yarn is available, see how difficult it is to pull apart into two strands. If it separates easily, the yarn was probably made in a factory, where machines stretch and align fibers so well that they run parallel. Handcarding and handspinning do not remove the natural curliness of fleece, and so it remains uneven in the yarn.

Buyers must also select from a wide variety of sizes although most weavers produce weavings that are two and a half feet by five feet because they are a popular size and economical to buy. Such weavings usually are not made with handspun wool or a double warp and may or may not be colorfast. Nevertheless, for the newly initiated they are a wonderful way to experiment with the exuberant colors and fanciful designs of Zapotec artistry.

Plate 37
Salvador Hipolito, 1998
Tres Flores y Greca
(Three Flowers and
Geometrics)
40 x 72 ins.

This unusual composition
combines an ancient glyph
border with a more mod-
ern central design. It is of
aniline dyes and handspun
wool yarns. Weaving cour-
tesy of Scott Roth.

Plate 38
Jesús Hernández, 1998
Relampagos (Lightening)
30 x 60 ins.

This is a common design made by many of Teotitlán's weavers in a multitude of color combinations.

Plate 39
Jesús Hernández, 1998
Untitled
30 x 60 ins.

This exuberant commercial
design is of aniline dyes
and factory yarn.

Plate 40
The Family of
Antonio Martínez, 1998
Diamantes y Maguey
(Diamonds and
Maguey Cactus)
30 x 60 ins.

Natural and aniline dyes
and handspun yarn were
used for this popular
design. The serrated dia-
mond is a universal pattern
seen in weavings all over
the world while the
"maguey" border has
been found throughout
Mexico dating back several
centuries.

Plate 41
Eligio Bazan, 1998
Estrella Nueva
30 x 60 ins.

An original design by Scott
Roth in undyed handspun
wool.

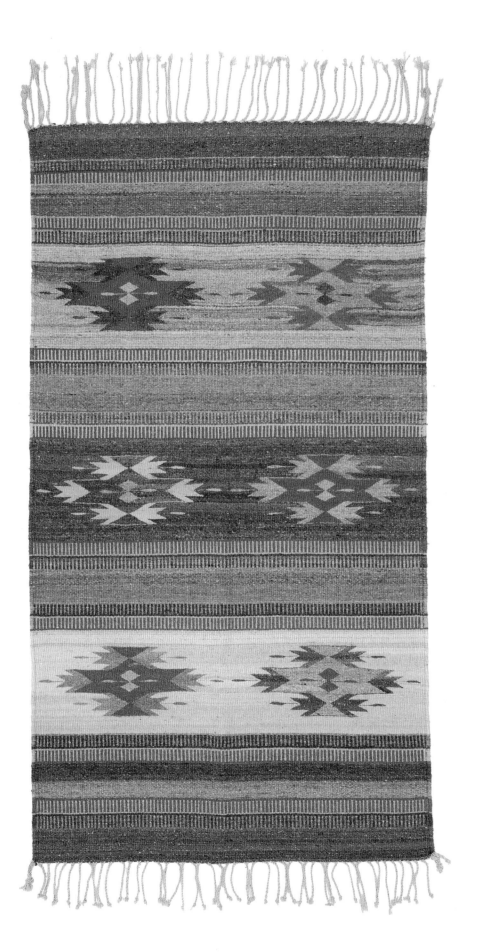

Plate 42
Eligio Bazan, 1996
Texcoco Natural
30 x 60 ins.

This pattern has been
in the weaver's family
for four generations.
Made from undyed
handspun wool.

Plate 43
Francisco Martínez, 1998
Untitled
39 x 79 ins.

The yarn for this weaving
was handspun in Teotítlan
and colored with natural
dyes. Weaving courtesy of
Thomas Foote.

Plate 44
Ponciano Hipolito, 1997
Pájaros y Flores
(Birds and Flowers)
63 x 76 ins.

This design was originated
by the weaver in the late
1960s. Aniline dyes and
handspun yarn were used.
Weaving courtesy of Scott
Roth.

CHAPTER SEVEN
NEW DIRECTIONS: INTERWEAVING TRADITION AND INNOVATION

Te otitlán's weavers typically produce two categories of rugs—those they consider "standard" and those that are "special." "Standard" rugs tend to be of factory-made wool and designs common to most weavers in the village, such as crosses, stars, or "Navajo clouds" coupled with simple or fancy stripes and "floating elements" originally created by Richard Enzer. The background tones of these rugs are produced when the weaver dyes yarn consisting of gray and cream wools spun in sequence. Since each absorbs the dye differently and yields a pronounced color striation, this overdyeing adds visual interest to relatively uncomplicated patterns.

Any novel or intricate pattern that requires more time, talent, and skill to create is considered "special." Such rugs are often of handspun wool. Patterns include bold geometric Navajo designs of the kind found in the 1988 book *Navajo Textiles: The William Randolph Hearst Collection* by Nancy J. Blomberg, a highly influential publication first introduced to Teotitecos by the North American importers in the 1980s, or complicated Navajo designs appropriated from other books and photographs. The real beauty of these rugs is the innovative use of color: Navajos prefer a limited color palette whereas Teotiteco weavers favor a wide range of creative color combinations.

Other patterns considered "special" are serrated diamonds (*Diamantes y Maguey*); "Tree of Life" designs with birds, animals, and flowers (*Arbol de la Vida, Mil Pájaros, Palomas*); renderings of famous paintings; depictions of prehistoric cave pictographs; and interpretations of pre-Columbian designs taken from ancient ruins, including the old glyphs located in the Teotitlán church. In recent years, uniquely Zapotec designs, such as *caracol* (snail) and *greca* (Greek key), are being revived by both importers and weavers. While importers appreciate the intricate, flowing lines of

Arnulfo Mendoza, one of Mexico's most acclaimed artists, revived the colonial-period *sarape* design and created original tapestries and paintings representing mythological forms and concepts from his Zapotec Indian heritage.

such rugs, the Zapotec value the rich heritage they reflect. In fact, many weavers say that, if the market supported them, they would not only focus on ancient designs but would create new, original work embodying personal ideas. One weaver who has been experimenting with new concepts is Arnulfo Mendoza, whose pieces are displayed at La Mano Mágica in Oaxaca City.

Mendoza has revitalized the nineteenth-century Saltillo *sarape* design of the diamond medallion shimmering against a speckled field. In earlier times, Oaxaca was a center of silk production and silk fibers were incorporated into *sarape* weavings, reputedly making them so delicate they could be pulled through a wedding ring. Mendoza's contemporary weavings of wool, cotton, and silk, combined with threads of silver and gold, are as detailed and finely rendered as those stunning antique textiles.

Mendoza first became interested in Saltillo *sarape* patterns in the mid-1980s after visiting museum exhibitions and perusing books on classic textiles. He was attracted to the technical refinement of these weavings, which embodied the elegance he wished to achieve in his own work. He says, "After spending time observing and absorbing the essence of the Saltillo *sarape*, I concluded that it was important to initiate a revitalization of those weavings of centuries past."

Further, drawing on his training at Oaxaca's Escuela de Bellas Artes (School of Fine Arts), studies in France and Japan, and impressions of the natural world, Mendoza has created a collection of innovative paintings and tapestries depicting mythic figures from his Zapotec heritage. The distinctive colors and images of one such weaving, *El Viaje Amoroso* (The Amorous Journey), were inspired by a fishing community his brother-in-law belonged to in the Pacific Northwest of Canada. He explains, "I wanted to create a testimony to the memory of all that I experienced there—the beauty and sensuality of the ocean and the deep love it caused me to feel." Indeed, the rich blues, browns, and oranges he uses, the way red blends into gold like a sunset, and the swirling pre-Columbian whorls reproduced in the ocean waves evoke the ambience of primordial seas. In this weaving Mendoza utilizes a technique called distressed warp whereby the warp is intentionally pulled tight in some areas and left loose in others, producing an irregular surface that gives the ocean waves form and dimension.

Another maverick in Teotitlán is Antonio Martínez, whose use of brilliant color is daring and whose quieter weavings are uniquely beautiful. Though other weavers sometimes employ designs similar to those of Martínez, few create tapestries of such magnificent colors. Whether dazzling or *suave* (soft), each of Martínez's textiles has an ingenious fusion of hues.

To further challenge his talent for color, most recently Martínez has been reviving design motifs from the small clay stamps used by his ancestors to decorate pottery, cloth, and paper. These stamps, shaped like cylinders, cones, or flat bars with handles, were typically dipped in dyes similar to those used by weavers today. The patterns they produced were simplified representations of animals, plants, flowers, and humans, combined with geometric elements. Martínez's jaguars and serpents bring to life these ancient, mysterious configurations so important to early Zapotec beliefs about the nature of life.

When questioned about his work, Martínez says, "It is important to me to create works of art that keep the traditions of my ancestors alive. The pre-Columbian designs I use are not necessarily popular, but I find them interesting. When I am designing and weaving them, it is like going to school because I am learning and discovering so many new ideas. My work is not only about making money to support my family but also to educate the people of Mexico about their cultural heritage. This is the greatest value."

Finally, a discussion of village innovators would be incomplete without mentioning the paterfamilias of Teotiteco weavers, Isaac Vásquez. Now in his sixties, he no longer weaves, but his past creations are exceptional for their inventiveness, gracefulness, and charm. In collaboration with Mexico's esteemed modern painters Francisco Toledo and Rufino Tamayo, Vásquez revived ancient methods for extracting dyes from natural sources, particularly reds from cochineal and blues from indigo, for which he is best known. In addition, he also contributed to Teotitlán's artistic heritage

An important figure among Teotiteco weavers, Isaac Vásquez (shown with his family) was once a maverick in his town. With Mexico's esteemed painters Francisco Toledo and Rufino Tamayo, Vásquez resurrected ancestral methods of extracting dyes from plants and insects. He also contributed to Teotitlán's artistic legacy by interpreting the imagery of his country's original citizens and transforming it into masterful tapestries.

opposite
Antonio Martínez, responsible for revitalizing ancient Mexican designs, also interprets modern paintings. Here he weaves a composition adapted from a painting by Paul Klee, first having drawn the design onto his warp threads.

by studying and interpreting the imagery of Mexico's indigenous people, transforming these designs into masterful tapestries (Peden 1991). For example, though at first glance the *caracol* (snail) design seems to be simply an interesting interlacing of geometric shapes, this ancient pattern was originally a profound conceptualization of the circularity of human existence. Vásquez explains, "The *caracol* symbolizes life itself. It starts in nothing and ends in nothing. It is a positive and negative construction with shapes that have no beginning and no end. It is continuous and unending."

Similarly, one of his weavings portraying a monkey actually tells the Mayan story of the miracle of creation. He remarks: "This is a representation of the joy and happiness that takes place in the world when a new being is born." Still another tapestry entitled *Ciencias Médicas* (Medical Sciences) depicts a patient's journey from waiting room to surgery to prayers for recovery, an interpretation of a deteriorated mural discovered in the 1930s. Using his prodigious imagination, Vásquez re-created the scene and lent it the purest of primary colors perhaps to convey the elemental quality of the patient's emotions. Says Vásquez, "In this weaving, you see a suggestion of words above a human heart. This is as if to say the patient is asking with all his heart to have his prayers heard by the gods and to be cured. You also see butterflies, which are considered spirit messengers, and these descend from the heavens to give the patient hope. Plants in the foreground are the doctors' healing tools, and the feet inside one of them indicate that that particular plant will enable the ailing patient to get back on his feet and resume his healthy life."

This desire to build on the past represents one more acknowledgment by the Zapotec people of their illustrious legacy. According to an importer in Colorado, Teotitecos are so dedicated to preserving their traditions that as many as half of the village's population resides in its U.S. sister city—Oxnard, California—in order to ease competition for money, living space, and farmland. However, although family members leave, they are never cut off from their community. Says Dennis Crawford of Marisol Imports, "If something happens in Teotitlán, an hour later everyone knows about it in Oxnard!"

In the vast and eclectic United States, people do not share a common ancestry, religion, or even language. We value individualism and distrust communal arrangements, yet the appeal of the Zapotecan way of life is vicariously soothing. The notion that individuals can achieve a peaceful and satisfying coexistence while preserving their ancient traditions is inspirational and provides hope for our own humanity.

Plate 45
The Family of
Antonio Martínez, 1998
Serpiente con Grecas
(Serpent with Geometrics)
39 x 62 ins.

This is an adaptation of a
prehistoric clay stamp.
The colors are natural and
aniline, and the yarn is
handspun.

Plate 46
Arnulfo Mendoza, 1996
Diamante (Diamond)
72 x 38 ins.

Inspired by 19th-century
Saltillo *sarapes*, this tapes-
try is of silk and wool with
gold and silver details.
Collection of Richard and
Holly Altman. Photo by
Marcela Taboada.

Plate 47
Arnulfo Mendoza, 1996
**Diamantes Entre
Diamantes**
(Diamonds Between
Diamonds)
55 x 87 ins.

This wool and silk weaving
is a perfect example of
Mendoza's revival of the
finest Saltillo *sarape*
designs. Collection of
Leopoldo Mendez. Photo
by Marcela Taboada.

Plate 48
Isaac Vásquez, 1977
Jaguar
40 x 60 ins.

In ancient Zapotec society, the jaguar was always associated with power. This fiercesome example is an original design of hand-spun wool and natural dyes. Weaving courtesy of Thomas Foote.

Plate 49
Isaac Vásquez, 1992
Ciencias Médicas (Medical Sciences)
48 x 70 ins.

This design is from a fourth-century mural near Teotihuacán. The red background is cochineal-dyed yarn. Weaving courtesy of Scott Roth.

Plate 50
The Family of
Antonio Martínez, 1998
Monos (Monkeys)
32 x 54 ins.

Based on ancient Mexican
designs, this tapestry is
made of natural dyes and
handspun yarn.

Plate 51
Antonio Martínez, 1998
Untitled
39 x 47 ins.

This is an adaptation of a
painting by Paul Klee. The
colors are from natural
dyes, and the yarn is
handspun.

Plate 52
Antonio Martínez, 1998
Diamantes (Diamonds)
48 x 84 ins.

Natural and aniline dyes
were used for this weav-
ing, as well as handspun
yarn. This is a common
design made unique with
the use of brilliant colors
and a Navajo-inspired
border.

ACKNOWLEDGMENTS

First and foremost, I wish to thank the weavers of Teotitlán and their families for their time, patience, and graciousness. Unfortunately, due to limitations of space only a few of the village's extraordinary weavers could be included in this book. Many more deserve recognition for their achievements.

I would like to express gratitude to Scott Roth, without whom much of this book could not have been written. Despite his hectic business schedule, he made every effort to provide research materials, introductions to weaving families, photography opportunities, and even his own collection of antique and contemporary rugs. With sensitivity, humor, and intelligence, he worked with me to ensure that this book accurately recounted the Zapotec weavers' story.

My sincere thanks to Mary Wachs of the Museum of New Mexico Press for appreciating the value of a book about Zapotec weavers, her willingness to take a chance on this project, and her recommendations that considerably improved the final outcome.

Thanks are also due to Mary Jane Gagnier de Mendoza, Mark Winter, Luisa Gelenter, Joyce Marcus, Marcela Taboada, Lynn Stephen, Claudine Colmenar of Arte Primitivo, Thomas Foote, and Marc Schmitt for their helpful information and suggestions. I am also grateful to my coach, Cheryl Gilman, for her expert advice and loving support, and to Marcia Yudkin for encouragement and editorial help. Special thanks to my friends and colleagues for their warm support. And finally to my family, I wish to express deep appreciation for their love and generosity throughout my life.

RESOURCES FOR
ZAPOTEC WEAVINGS

Shops where Zapotec rugs are bought and sold.

Anomaly Imports
Santa Barbara, California
(805) 687-8830

Arizona Creations
Scottsdale, Arizona
(602) 595-9782

Catherine Lane Interiors
Livingston, Montana
(406) 222-7166

Decor Southwest
Lakewood, Colorado
(800) 417-5457

Eagle Dancer
Santa Fe, New Mexico
(505) 986-2055

The Kaibab Shops
Tucson, Arizona
(520) 795-6905

Marisol Imports
Boulder, Colorado
(303) 442-3142

Mountain Comfort
Park City, Utah
(435) 647-5880

Packard's
Santa Fe, New Mexico
(505) 983-9241

Santa Fe Connection
Overland Park, Kansas
(913) 642-7275

Santa Fe Interiors
Santa Fe, New Mexico
(800) 877-4784

Santa Fe Savvy
Scottsdale, Arizona
(602) 483-1444

Scott Roth
Claremont, California
(909) 621-1019

Skyfire
Jerome, Arizona
(520) 634-8081

Southern Exposure
Mystic, Connecticut
(860) 572-1007

Southwest Weavers
Stow, Massachusetts
(800) 955-4194

Squaw Valley Trading Post-Zapotecs
Olympic Valley, California
(530) 583-6468

TOKLAT Gallery
Aspen, Colorado
(970) 925-7345

Two Grey Hills Gallery
Jackson, Wyoming
(307) 733-2677

Viva Southwest
Las Vegas, Nevada
(702) 887-0770

Weeds Gallery
Monticello, Utah
(435) 587-2601

White Buffalo
Truckee, California
(530) 587-4446

Zapotec Art
Houston, Texas
(713) 529-0890

La Unica Cosa
Taos, New Mexico
(800) 748-1756

BIBLIOGRAPHY

Blomberg, Nancy J. *Navajo Textiles: The William Randolph Hearst Collection.* Tucson and London: University of Arizona Press, 1988.

de Avila, Alejandro. Personal communication. 1998.

Gelenter, Luisa. Personal communication. 1998.

Jeter, James, and Paula Marie Juelke. The Saltillo Sarape: An Exhibition Organized by the Santa Barbara Museum of Art. Santa Barbara, Calif.: New World Arts, 1978.

Klein, Kathryn, ed. *The Unbroken Thread: Conserving the Textile Traditions of Oaxaca.* Los Angeles: Getty Conservation Institute, 1997.

Marcus, Joyce, and Kent V. Flannery. *Zapotec Civilization: How Urban Society Evolved in Mexico's Oaxaca Valley.* London: Thames and Hudson, 1996.

Mendoza, Mary Jane Gagnier de. Personal communication. 1998.

Miller, Robert Ryal. *Mexico: A History.* Norman: University of Oklahoma Press, 1985.

Peden, Margaret Sayers. *Out of the Volcano.* Washington, D.C. and London: Smithsonian Institution Press, 1991.

Rodee, Marian E. *One Hundred Years of Navajo Rugs.* Albuquerque: University of New Mexico Press, 1995.

Ross, Gary N. "The Bug in the Rug." *Natural History* (March 1986) 66–72.

Roth, Scott. Personal communication. 1998.

Sabloff, Jeremy A. *The Cities of Ancient Mexico: Reconstructing a Lost World.* New York: Thames and Hudson, 1997.

Sayer, Chloe. *Mexican Textiles.* London: British Museum Publications, 1985.

Selby, Henry A. *Zapotec Deviance: The Convergence of Folk and Modern Sociology.* Austin and London: University of Texas Press, 1974.

Stephen, Lynn. *Zapotec Women.* Austin and London: University of Texas Press, 1991.

Toledo, Francisco. Personal communication. 1998.

Vásquez, Isaac. Personal communication. 1998.

Whitecotton, Joseph W. *The Zapotecs: Princes, Priests and Peasants.* Norman: University of Oklahoma Press, 1977.

Winter, Mark. Personal communication. 1998.